ST

WHAT IT MEANS TO BE A
CHRISTIAN

David C. Cook Publishing Co.
ELGIN, ILLINOIS/WESTON, ONTARIO

Note: Some of the material in this book originally appeared under the title, *Getting into God* by Stuart Briscoe.

Published by David C. Cook Publishing Co.
850 N. Grove Ave., Elgin, IL 60120
Cable address: DCCOOK

Curriculum Editor: John Duckworth
Designer: Catherine Hesz Colten
Cover Illustrator: Miriam Schottland
Printed in U.S.A.
Library of Congress Catalog Card Number 86-71794
ISBN: 1-55513-803-9

CONTENTS

▼

INTRODUCTION

▼

Years ago, in England, I joined the Marines—not out of choice, but compulsion. Arriving at the barracks gates, I found myself both elated and uneasy. The prospects of being a real, live Marine were exciting to a young, red-blooded kid who knew no better. Yet the strangeness of it all made me wonder: What would I have to do? Would I be able to do it?

The first few days served only to confirm my worst suspicions. I had little idea of what was going on. Getting "kitted out," for example, was one experience I will never forget. We were marched into a long shed which had a counter stretching the length of one wall. Behind the counter stood men who turned out to be geniuses; with scarcely a glance at us as we moved past, they estimated our size, tastes, and abnormalities, and hurled piles of strange uniforms and equipment in our direction.

We caught the stuff as best we could and emerged from the shed "weary and heavy laden." As we looked at our newly acquired possessions, we hadn't a clue as to what they were for, where they went, or what we were supposed to do with them. I didn't know whether to put them on my back, drape them 'round my neck, suspend them from my stomach, eat them, polish them, or salute them!

New Christians sometimes feel the same way. Excited about their life-changing experience, they find themselves deluged with supplies and situations that are strange and vaguely disquieting: big, black Bibles, shiny and obviously new; hymnbooks

7

full of odd tunes fitted to odd phrases describing a "rock of ages," a "fountain of blood," and "showers of blessing"; prayer lists of "the Lord's servants" somewhere "on the foreign field" who "covet our prayers." And ominous bundles of little envelopes!

Terminology was a problem in those early Marine days, too. We were told to develop *esprit de corps*, but none of us knew what it was. Phrases were repeated with great solemnity, but one had the distinct impression there was not too much communication involved. One instructor, for instance, insisted that we learn the phrase "to facilitate fragmentation"—which was the answer he required to the question, "Why does a hand grenade have grooves?"

The terms a new Christian faces are no less confusing. After all, in many Christian circles there are no men and women, just "brethren" and "sisters"; people don't die, they are "called home"; the "will of God" and the "Word of God" sound almost the same, as do "apostle" and "epistle"; and the difference between I and II Chronicles and I and II Corinthians can easily be missed.

In all fairness to the Marines, I must say that eventually they taught us their terms and where all the equipment went. In time we began to function properly, and for this I was grateful.

The aim of this book is to do something similar for Christians, both new and not so new, who feel a need for instruction in some basic practicalities of Christian experience. Its aim is to help us discover what being a Christian means—in everyday, down-to-earth terms. Whether you're a new or "old" believer, or a "seeker" who's considering Christ from a bit of a distance, join us!

Stuart Briscoe

CHAPTER 1

▼

WHY I AM
A CHRISTIAN

by Stuart

After hearing me preach, a man told me he thought I was an excellent salesman. I told him I obviously wasn't, since I hadn't gotten my message across to him. Had he heard me properly, he would have realized I wasn't *selling* anything—I was trying to give it away!

Many people are like that man. They think Christianity was designed by God for their benefit, and that preachers spend their lives trying to persuade people to "buy into" it. In a sense this is true. But God designed Christianity because it was something He wanted to *share* with mankind.

What Is a Christian?
Before we go further, a definition of "Christian" seems necessary. A Christian is a person who has a relationship with Christ. He or she belongs to Christ, is identified with Christ in much the same way that an Asian is related to Asia or a musician is identified by his music. Christ being who He is—the eternal Son of God—there is no difficulty seeing that mere humans are highly privileged to have a relationship with Him. They also accept the fact that the relationship must be on His terms, not theirs.

Herein lies a problem for some people. They feel they can be Christians without relating to Christ on His terms. They profess Christianity but know little of what Christ taught, less of what He promised, and even less of what He requires. Their declarations are highly suspect, and they should carefully examine Christ's claims and demands.

Christ taught that God the Father had sent Him into the world to bring people into a harmony with God which they had once enjoyed but lost. To do this, He had to die on the cross for sin, be buried to show the reality of His death, and rise again from the dead to demonstrate God's acceptance of His sacrifice and His victory over sin, death, and hell.

It was on the basis of this teaching that Christ was free to make His demands. First, He demanded *repentance*. He left no illusions in people's minds as to what He felt about sin; He expected them to call it sin and turn from it. Second, He insisted on *faith*—faith and dependence that stopped trusting anything or anyone but Himself for blessing and meaning. Third, He talked forcefully of making repentance and faith visible through *commitment* to Him and what He was doing.

This kind of commitment gladly acknowledges and accepts Christ's authority—which can mean going where it's hard to go and doing what is hard to do. But there is a resource to help in these difficult situations: the Holy Spirit. It is He—the third member of the Trinity—who lives in the repentant, dependent, committed Christian. He is there to stimulate, clarify, strengthen, encourage, and where necessary, prick the conscience. He keeps the Christian moving toward deeper discoveries of what God wants to do.

In addition to this remarkable spiritual resource, God has given us many helps—including the Bible, prayer, fellowship, and the Church. All are intended to aid the Christian in becoming what God wants him or her to be.

Drawn by His Desire

But why should we care what God wants us to be? Indeed, why be a Christian at all?

We should become Christians not only because there's "something in it for me," but also because there is something in it for God. As for me, I am a Christian because of the inestimable benefits I derive from being a child of God—and because I am convinced Christianity is true. But I am also a Christian because I believe the Lord *desires, deserves,* and *demands* my allegiance.

"Now, hold on," you might say. "Why would God, who obviously has so much on His mind, desire *anything* from a miniscule part of the cosmos like you?"

My answer: Because He made me uniquely capable of knowing and enjoying Him—and it grieves Him deeply that we have been estranged.

As a human being, I have been made in a way that allows me to know God. When I become alienated from Him, I no longer function to the limits of my ability. I am then like a fish out of water. Fish were created to function in water, and when they are removed from it, they cannot manuever or even live for long. Similarly, birds do well in the air—but when caged, they rarely exercise their flying skills. I, like the rest of humanity, was made to function in the environment of God's presence; when I lose Him I become a fish out of water, a bird in a cage.

God does not like that. He longs to lead me back to fellowship with Him—the fellowship of which I am capable, for which I was created, and in which He delights. He wonderfully demonstrated this desire through Christ, who in His earthly life repeatedly reached out to men and women of all stripes and warmly embraced them in His love.

He displayed this same love when He went out of His way to gather disciples. He wanted them to be with Him. He told them how much He wanted to share with them, and on special occasions He relaxed with His friends Martha, Mary, and Lazarus. Even on the cross Christ reached out to a fellow sufferer and promised that they would shortly share Paradise.

When I discovered that Christ extended a similar love to *all* people including me, I was overwhelmed. This compelling desire of His to share His life with me has drawn me to Him. It is part of the reason why I am a Christian.

Responding to His Rescue

I have also been deeply affected as I've discovered how far God was willing to go to allow people like me to participate in His plan. For God and me to be reconciled, it was necessary to remove the barrier I'd put between us. That barrier was made of blatant disobedience toward Him and disrespectful disregard for His purposes for me. On top of that was a towering load of guilt and the certainty of divine judgment.

Nothing I could do would begin to remove that barrier. But God took the initiative and did the work Himself. The removal cost Christ His life in a most dramatic and traumatic manner. His motivation was love, and His kind of love deserves a response. I gladly and willingly offer that response to Him.

Such is the winsomeness of Christ that we tend to overlook His awesome majesty. He is Lord of all! In fact, it is only in His capacity as Lord that He is powerful and authoritative enough to offer salvation. If He is not Lord over death, how can He deliver from it? If the grave still holds Him, how can He offer to take me through the grave and into the presence of His Father?

If Christ is Lord, He must be acknowledged as Lord. Everything about Him—His life, death, resurrection, miracles, and claims spoke volumes about His deity and authority. I need to come to Him, therefore, with a sense of humble submission— which is the only appropriate response to a Lord who not only invites but also commands.

Even if I had not been drawn by His desire for fellowship with me, or felt compelled to respond positively to His love for me, I would still be a Christian because Christ demands my allegiance by virtue of His Lordship. I'm glad that He did more than just demand it; but even if He hadn't, I would be hard put to think of a reason why He should not have it!

CHAPTER 2

▼

BECOMING
A CHRISTIAN
by Jill

The pretty, dark-haired girl in the hospital bed next to me smiled. It reminded me of the dawn breaking after a dark, dark night. After all, I was sick and far from home—and never having been in the hospital before, I was frightened and not a little lonely.

"Hello! What's up?" she said cheerfully.

I willingly responded, glad for a listening ear. "What a lot of forms you have to fill in," I complained, referring to the red tape I'd had to wade through on being checked into the hospital. "Why do they want to know your life history? They even asked me what *religion* I was!"

Quietly she asked what my answer had been. "I said *Christian*," I replied. "Everyone's a Christian in England, aren't they?"

There was silence for a moment. "No," she said finally. "They're not."

"What do you mean, they're not?"

"You're not a Christian just because you live in England," she answered.

"You're *not?*" I asked, incredulous.

She laughed. "What's your name?"

"Jill."

"Mine's Janet. Why don't you read this? It may clear up a bit of confusion for you." She handed me a booklet entitled *Becoming a Christian*.

15

Becoming a Christian? I thought. *How can I become something I already am?*

During the days that followed, I read that booklet many times. It was very simple and told me four things about myself that I did not know.

All Have Sinned

First, I learned that I was a sinner. Janet explained to me that God had already examined me and found me sadly lacking. He had published my grade—a failing one—in His Book, the Bible. Janet handed me a Bible and encouraged me to read the following verses:

> All have sinned and fall short of the glory of God (Romans 3:23, NIV).

> What shall we conclude then? Are we any better? Not at all! We have already made the charge that Jews and Gentiles alike are all under sin. As it is written: "There is no one righteous, not even one" (Romans 3:9, 10, NIV).

> We all, like sheep, have gone astray, each of us has turned to his own way; and the Lord has laid on him the iniquity of us all (Isaiah 53:6, NIV).

> The fool says in his heart, "There is no God." They are corrupt, their deeds are vile; there is no one who does good. The Lord looks down from heaven on the sons of men to see if there are any who understand, any who seek God. All have turned aside, they have together become corrupt; there is no one who does good, not even one (Psalm 14:1-3, NIV).

It all made good sense. Only perfect people could go to Heaven—or it wouldn't be Heaven for very long!

The Wages of Sin

Second, Janet told me that sinners cannot go to Heaven unforgiven. She explained that actions have consequences, and we are responsible for our behavior and moral choices. God sees everything we do, and our sin must be punished. Janet showed me Hebrews 9:27 (NIV): "Man is destined to die once, and after that to face judgment." I will never forget reading that verse and realizing that even though we might think we can get away with sin "down here," we will find there's nowhere to hide after our lives are over.

The following verses applied as well:

Sin entered the world through one man, and death through sin, and in this way death came to all men, because all sinned (Romans 5:12, NIV).

What man can live and not see death, or save himself from the power of the grave? (Psalm 89:48, NIV)

The soul who sins is the one who will die (Ezekiel 18:4, NIV).

The mind of sinful man is death (Romans 8:6, NIV).

After desire has conceived, it gives birth to sin; and sin, when it is full-grown, gives birth to death (James 1:15, NIV).

Like water spilled on the ground, which cannot be recovered, so we must die (II Samuel 14:14, NIV).

Jesus Died for Us

Third, the booklet informed me that Jesus had died to do something about my sinful state. Janet asked whether I believed Jesus loved me and wanted to forgive me. She explained that

Christ had taken my place on the cross as my substitute. I came to understand that God's Son had willingly come to earth to make possible my escape from God's anger at my sin. Verse after verse of Scripture convinced me that this was not some "cultish" idea I was hearing; it was the truth:

> For God so loved the world that he gave his one and only Son, that whoever believes in him shall not perish but have eternal life (John 3:16, NIV).

> For you know that it was not with perishable things such as silver or gold that you were redeemed . . . but with the precious blood of Christ, a lamb without blemish or defect (I Peter 1:18, 19, NIV).

> But God demonstrates his own love for us in this: While we were still sinners, Christ died for us (Romans 5:8, NIV).

> But he was pierced for our transgressions, he was crushed for our iniquities; the punishment that brought us peace was upon him, and by his wounds we are healed (Isaiah 53:5, NIV).

> But we see Jesus . . . now crowned with glory and honor because he suffered death, so that by the grace of God he might taste death for everyone (Hebrews 2:9, NIV).

> Christ died for sins once for all, the righteous for the unrighteous, to bring you to God. He was put to death in the body but made alive by the Spirit (I Peter 3:18, NIV).

Accept the Gift

Fourth, I learned that I needed to accept the gracious gift of eternal life. "Do you believe all this, Jill?" Janet asked me.

"Yes," I replied truthfully. "But now what?" I needed and wanted Christ, but just how to put everything together was a mystery to me. I felt foolish not knowing, but my new friend put my mind at ease.

"I didn't know how to receive Christ either," she confided. "Someone had to help me. I'd like to help you, too, if you'd like me to."

"Please," I whispered.

"Why don't I say a simple prayer of invitation that you can make your own?" she suggested. We bowed our heads right then and there in the hospital; I was discovering that you can meet God anywhere, wherever you are. In the moments that followed, I echoed Janet's words as she prayed something like this: "Dear Jesus, I understand I am the sinner You died to save. Thank You for dying for me. Please come into my heart and be my Savior. Give me Your Holy Spirit. Thank You for coming in as You promised. Amen."

Immediately Janet turned to Revelation 3:20 in her Bible and instructed me to read it out loud to her: "Here I am! I stand at the door and knock. If anyone hears my voice and opens the door, I will come in and eat with him, and he with me" (Revelation 3:20, NIV).

"Does He say He will come in?" Janet asked.

"Yes," I replied.

"Then He has," Janet assured me. "He always does what He says."

It was done! The great exchange was complete. I had given my life to Christ, and He had given His life to me! I eagerly read the rich promises that I knew had become mine:

Assurance of forgiveness: "If we confess our sins, he is faithful and just and will forgive us our sins and purify us from all unrighteousness" (I John 1:9, NIV).

Assurance of eternal life: "Whoever believes in him shall not perish but have eternal life" (John 3:16, NIV).

Assurance of provision: "Are not five sparrows sold for two pennies? Yet not one of them is forgotten by God. . . . Don't be afraid; you are worth more than many sparrows" (Luke 12:6, 7, NIV).

Soon I was well again. Out of the hospital, I found myself back at college among my friends. I had entered the hospital an extremely sick young woman in body—and in soul. Now I was back where I belonged, healthy and whole and ready to discover my world in a brand-new way.

"Therefore, if anyone is in Christ, he is a new creation; the old has gone, the new has come!" (II Corinthians 5:17, NIV). Hallelujah—it was so!

CHAPTER 3

▼

STUDYING THE BIBLE: WHY BOTHER?

by Stuart

Once I joined a newly opened local library. The woman who looked after my enrollment was proud of the facility and offered to show me around. But I was in a hurry, and insisted I could find my way around, get the material I needed, and be on my way. It might have been wiser to accept her offer, though, for when I got among the well-stocked shelves I was utterly lost!

That brings me to the Bible. Whatever else the Bible is, it is a library. If you like statistics, you may be interested to know it contains 66 books, 1,189 chapters, 23,214 verses, and 773,692 words in the *King James Version*. That provides plenty of places in which to get lost, and that's exactly what many people have done.

In that case, you might ask, why venture into the Bible at all? Is it worth risking confusion just to find your way around what some people feel is an "outmoded" book? In other words, why should a Christian bother to study the Bible?

Let's be practical about Bible study. In order to really benefit from it, *you have to be motivated.* You have to *want* to study it. Unfortunately, some people haven't even come this far. They assume that listening to a sermon once in a while is sufficient. But they are wrong. It is important that each Christian learn to feed himself or herself from the Word of God.

A few years ago some friends invited me to go to the opera. As I was their guest and they had a box for a performance of *Eugene Onegin*, I was happy to go with them. But it wasn't the

21

greatest evening I've ever spent. The leading soprano was a formidable-looking lady who sang in a way that seemed to intimidate the rather small tenor who was supposed to sweep her off her feet. The opera was sung in Polish and Russian—so I was told—for it was being performed in Prague, Czechoslovakia. Frankly, I got a little bored. I would have been happy to leave after the first act because I had no idea what was happening.

What people don't understand, they don't appreciate. I believe many people aren't motivated to study the Bible because they don't understand its significance and importance—just as I didn't understand the opera.

Let me point out four important facts concerning the Bible:

1. *The Bible is inspired by the Holy Spirit.* This means the Spirit, a member of the Holy Trinity, moved people to write what He wanted them to write—so we would know what God thinks (see II Peter 1:21 and II Timothy 3:16).

Most things we know are the product of human research or thinking. But humanity has been proven wrong quite a few times, so we all know we have to treat those findings with care. *If only God would tell us what's going on,* we think. *Then we could have some confidence and build our lives on what He said.* That's exactly what God has done in the Bible. Many times we read in it phrases like, "Thus saith the Lord. . . ." or "He spoke with authority. . . ." or "Hear what the Spirit says. . . ." This is exciting, for it means that people living on a tiny planet in the Twentieth Century can know what God thinks about things and what He plans to do.

2. *The Bible is the only way of knowing how to be reconciled to God.* Many people know something about God and would urgently like to know Him better than they do. But their knowledge is fuzzy, and they don't know which way to go or where to start looking for information. Paul said it is the Scriptures that make us "wise unto salvation" (II Timothy 3:15). That being the case, Christians should be highly motivated to research all they can about salvation in the only place they can find the information.

3. *The Bible is the only place to find out how to continue in the*

Christian life. "Where do we go from here?" is a popular query, though some of the answers offered in today's world are none too good. The same Bible passage (II Timothy 3:16, 17) that tells us God's Word is inspired and opens our eyes to salvation also tells us we need the Bible to become "equipped for every good work" (NIV). These verses also give us a few insights into how this takes place: through teaching, reproof, and correction. Teaching tells you what to do; reproof tells what not to do; correction tells you what to do when you have done what you were told not to do. And that covers just about everything!

4. *The Bible is the only place to discover what will happen in the future.* More and more people are studying horoscopes, visiting mediums, and reading science fiction because of an almost morbid interest in the future. But there is only one authoritative voice about the future—the Bible. Through the Bible alone we can know what lies ahead, what the world is coming to, what happens after death. The best that mere mortals can produce is speculation; the Bible offers revelation.

If you have never been moved to study the Bible before, consider those four vital facts. When understood, they become vital motivators. There are other reasons to look into God's Word, but these four should be sufficient to nudge a believer to read, mark, learn, and inwardly digest Scripture. If you are a Christian and still find yourself asking, "Why bother?" when it comes to Bible study, ask God for the understanding and desire to read His Word.

In the next two chapters we'll look at materials and methods of Bible study. First, however, I must give you a caution. Two ingredients are so necessary to Bible study that if they are missing, no materials or methods can make our study profitable.

The first of these ingredients is *our attitude toward Scripture.* Some people approach the Bible as a masterpiece of literary achievement, which it certainly is. Others love its poetry (and so they should), while still others revel in its historical detail (and well they might). But the Bible will yield little of eternal, life-changing value if it is approached purely as a literary or historical document. What really counts is the attitude that study of the Word of God leads us into truth. There is literary beauty and historical data in the Bible, but above all this there is eternal truth to be found nowhere else. Therefore the approach of the most learned theologian as well as the most humble reader must be one of reverent anticipation—expecting God to speak through the pages of His Word.

This brings us to the second ingredient. When you study, *pray.* Ask the Holy Spirit who inspired the Bible to interpret it to your own understanding. I know of no better prayer with which to approach Bible study than "Open thou mine eyes, that I may behold wondrous things out of thy law" (Psalm 119:18).

CHAPTER 4

STUDYING THE BIBLE:
TOOLS FOR DIGGING

by Stuart

Let's say you've been motivated to study the Bible. What do you need next? Some *materials*—tools for digging out the truth.

Atop your list of tools must come the Bible itself. "But that's so *obvious*," you say. Still, I am amazed at the number of people who don't seem to think the Bible is necessary for their study of it. They remind me of the Welshman who, when the ball was lost in the middle of a fiery rugby match, said, "Don't bother about the ball. Get on with the game!" There's as much chance of a good Bible study without a Bible as there is of a good rugby match without a ball.

In the English-speaking world we have so many editions of the Bible to choose from that some people become confused. Two basic kinds of versions are available—those that seek to be strict translations of the original Greek and Hebrew texts, and others that give the sense by way of paraphrase.

The difference between the paraphrase and translation is rather similar to the difference between a photograph and a watercolor sketch. The photo is exact in every detail, while the sketch captures the truth of the subject without all the detail. A paraphrase Bible is often easier to read than a more strict translation, so I use the former for general reading and the latter for detailed study. The former gives me an overview of what the Bible is saying, but the latter gives me material from which I can make a careful study.

Which should you have? For general reading I recommend

The Living Bible. For study you might try either a *King James Version* (he didn't write it, but commissioned its translation in 1611) or the *New American Standard Bible* or the *New International Version.* There are many others, but we'll settle for those for now. Eventually you may become like me and find you can't resist buying a copy of all of them!

The important thing about your Bible is that if you are going to study it, the print must be big enough. This is an elementary point, but necessary because many Bibles have apparently been designed more for beauty than use. It also helps if there is a margin in which to make some notes, and you may even wish to invest in a loose-leaf Bible. This is designed with removable pages—not so you can get rid of the bits you don't like without spoiling your Bible, but so you can write lots of notes on the paper provided and then fit them in at the right place!

It's not always necessary to purchase a large, expensive, new Bible. There are usually some available in secondhand bookstores, and you can buy a half-dozen quite inexpensively. Then you can give some to your friends and get them studying, too!

Next you need a notebook. Unless you have a loose-leaf Bible, you will need something in which to keep the products of your study. Nothing ornate is required; in fact, the simpler the notebook, the better. The main point is to preserve your great thoughts and discoveries. Another good reason to use a notebook is to make sure you're actually studying. Ever notice how easy it is to read something without thinking about it? You can't do that if you're taking notes, because you have to think about what to write down as you are reading. If, when you are through reading, there is a blank page looking at you from your notebook, you know something is wrong—and you go back and read until you have something to record.

You may find it helpful to mark each page with the day's date and enter something daily. This is one of the best ways I know to keep reading every day, because it gets embarrassing to see nothing entered from June 1 to July 13! Moreover, it's always good to be able to look back over the years and see how your understanding has grown.

26

Then you must have a concordance. This is a glorified index of the Bible. A complete concordance lists every word in the Bible alphabetically, and under each word a reference is given for every place that word appears. This is clearly helpful. Suppose you wanted to show someone how much God loved the world, but you couldn't remember John 3:16. You could turn to the word *love* and look at every reference until you found it. There is another good thing about a concordance; if you start looking under *love*, you will be amazed at how many times the word is used. You might just curl up on the rug with your Bible, notebook, and concordance and do a study on the subject.

There are various styles of concordances. Some Bibles have a small one in the back next to the maps, but you should save up and buy a big one. The most famous are *Young's*, *Strong's*, and *Cruden's*. Sometimes people ask me which would be best for them. I usually tell them, "If you're young, *Young's*; if you're strong, *Strong's*; and if you're crude, *Cruden's*." Don't worry, *Cruden's* fans—that's just a joke.

You also can make good use of a box of colored pencils. These can be used to draw pretty pictures on the church bulletin during boring sermons, but this is not their primary purpose! I have found it helpful to have a system of marking my Bible, not only as a means of making things stick in my memory as I mark them, but also as a way of finding information later. Now, don't get carried away at this point. There is a limit to the colors available, so you must limit your system to relatively few subjects. The idea is to choose a different color to stand for each topic. In my study, I use red to mark passages related to salvation, blue for Christian experience, green for the Holy Spirit, black for sin and judgment, orange for Heaven and the life to come, brown for God the Father, and terra-cotta (brownish orange) for the Son.

There is nothing magic about this system, but it certainly can be a help. One day I arrived at a church to discover I'd been advertised to give a talk on "The Holy Spirit in Galatians." That was great—except that nobody had told me. Nevertheless, I was not helpless. I just looked for the green lines neatly drawn under every reference to the Holy Spirit and explained each passage to the people.

When you mark your Bible, don't try to make it look like a Van Gogh painting. The less color you use, the better, as long as a neat, easy-to-see line is drawn under the relevant words. Marking in ink is usually not a good idea, since (1) the ink may go through the paper, and (2) whenever you turn to a page in your Bible you may tend to look at the uninspired notes before the inspired text. If you make your notes in ink, you may spend 20 years reading the same comments every time you turn to a page, but pencil can be changed. In fact, you'll probably discover that penciled notes gradually wear away—and by the time they do, it's time you thought of something new!

The materials I have listed—Bible, notebook, concordance, and pencils—are minimum requirements. If you wish to add another tool, I recommend a Bible dictionary, handbook, or encyclopedia. There are several available, ranging from small, compact books like *Halley's Bible Handbook* through the comprehensive *New Bible Dictionary* up to the five-volume *Zondervan Pictorial Encyclopedia of the Bible*. Examine some of these at your nearest Christian bookstore, and you will discover how valuable they can be to a fuller understanding of the Bible.

You may also want to purchase a commentary on the Bible. I have some reservations about the one-volume variety, since they are obviously limited by space; just printing the Bible itself *without* comments constitutes a large volume. Therefore comments in such books are necessarily sparse and often seem to deal with the parts in which you don't need help, referring you to another, more detailed book in problem areas! Still, you need to start somewhere in building your resource library, so ask your Christian bookstore to show you a variety of commentaries.

A word of warning: Dictionaries and commentaries are supposed to be *aids* to study, not *substitutes* for study. Some people can't be bothered to dig for themselves; they just grab what someone else has found and use that. Don't fall into this trap. You will benefit more from truths you discover through your own reading than from reading what someone else has said. The time to use a commentary comes when you can't understand what Scripture means at a certain point and need the help of a gifted teacher.

Shortly after I became a pastor, a woman asked me a question about the Bible which I couldn't answer. I told her, "I haven't the remotest idea" (one of my most frequent answers).

She was somewhat taken aback. "Would you find out for me, please?" she asked.

"No," I said, which left her even more taken aback. I explained that I would have to research it, and she was as capable of doing that as I was. Furthermore, if she researched it herself, it would be much more meaningful to her—and she could give the information to me.

The following week she told me she had not been very pleased with me, but had done as I suggested. The result was that she really had become enthusiastic about her own study. When a friend of hers asked her a question, she told her what I had said—and they *both* got into their Bibles for themselves!

We must not be lazy about digging into the Bible for ourselves. Using the right tools, we can come up with God's answers to our most heartfelt questions.

CHAPTER 5

▼

STUDYING THE BIBLE: THREE WAYS

by Stuart

Many books have been written about methods of Bible study; it's a big subject. In this chapter I'll describe three prominent ways to study God's Word.

A Book Study

The first method is to choose a *book* of the Bible and read it. Then read it again. If you have two versions, read one and then the other. When you have read it two or three times, you'll start to feel familiar with its overall content. Think of a title you would give the book.

Read the book still another time and look for its natural divisions. These can be discovered through careful attention to the subject matter; when the subject changes, you can detect the division. Sometimes sections are introduced by words like *but* or *nevertheless* or *therefore*. These words are often overlooked when people study the Bible, but to do so is to miss the point of much of Scripture. The word *but* shows the other side of a situation; *therefore* is usually there to apply what has just been said. When the Bible teaches a great truth, it often says, "Therefore do such and such a thing." As you continue your studies you will discover more of these seemingly unimportant words that make a big difference.

After you have divided the book into its natural divisions, give each division a title of your choosing. This will help to fix it in your mind and give you a brief summary of the contents of the passage. Now look at each division with your title in mind, making a note of everything the passage says about the subject you have decided is the central point. This is also known as the *inductive* method of study.

I used this approach when, as a young man, I was transferred to a new town by the bank that employed me. Feeling a little strange, I checked into my hotel on the first day and settled down to read my Bible. That day I turned to Psalm 1. I read through it two or three times and was struck by the fact that the psalm is basically a description of a "blessed man." I knew that blessed meant happy, so I wrote in my notebook, "The Happy Man." You can see what an exciting study this was for me at the time! I looked for the natural divisions and gave each one a title relating to the happy man. My notebook soon looked something like this:

The Happy Man: Psalm 1
1. His path . . . three things he avoids (v.1)
2. His pleasure . . . meditation in God's Law (v.2)
3. His position . . . like a tree by the river (v. 3a)
4. His productivity . . . bringing forth fruit (v. 3b)
5. His progress . . . his unwithering leaf, evergreen (v. 3c)
6. His prosperity . . . whatever he does (v. 3d)
7. His peace . . . the Lord knows his way (v. 6)

You will notice that I suffer from alliteration, but you mustn't let that bother you. Sometimes it helps to have different points begin with the same letter—and sometimes they won't fit that way however hard you try!

This is what I call a skeleton outline. As bodies are nicer than skeletons, it is necessary to put flesh on the bones. Take the first point, "His path." Note three things that verse 1 says about the path of the happy man, and ponder these. This example from the Psalms may prompt you to start a study of that book. This may be a little long for you, and you may become discouraged before you finish. But at least you could work on a *few* psalms.

Or you might like to try Philippians. I'll give you a start with the first chapter. When I began to study this chapter, I observed that Paul talked a lot about himself. That was exciting to me; I had become so enthralled with Paul that I wanted to know as much as possible about him. So my notes were as follows:

Paul with the Lid Off: Philippians 1
1. Greeting (vss. 1, 2)
2. Paul's delight (vss. 3-8)
3. Paul's desire (vss. 9-11)
4. Paul's devotion (vss. 12-21)
5. Paul's dilemma (vss. 22-26)
6. Paul's demands (vss. 27-30)

I began to fill in the details under each heading, and a profitable study followed.

A Word Study

Another way to study the Bible is to study a *word*. It's a long step from a book to a word—but to study a chapter, phrase, or sentence is to come eventually to a word study. This is much more interesting and important than it sounds at first.

If you look back at the outline I did for the first chapter of Philippians, you'll note that I called the first two verses "Greeting." You may decide, "Nothing very interesting there," and move on to verse 3. But look again. A number of words there deserve close scrutiny:

1. Servants
2. Saints
3. Bishops
4. Deacons
5. Grace
6. Peace

I am sure you know what all those words mean, but do you perceive the *depth* of meaning in each of them? Let's take the word *servant*. Look in a concordance or Bible dictionary to find

33

the meaning in the Biblical sense. *Young's Concordance* says *servant* is a translation of the Greek word *doulos*, which also means *slave*. Think of that! The word Paul uses to describe himself is the word *slave*. He thinks of himself as Christ's slave!

Or how about the word *saint?* Most people think a saint is someone in a stained-glass window with a thing like a dinner plate behind his head. Look in your reference book. *Young's Concordance* says the Greek word *hagios* means *saint, set apart, separate, holy.* Nothing to do with dinner plates or windows. A saint is someone really set apart for God.

The word *grace* is so remarkable that whole books have been written about it. It is one of the great words of our faith, and I must restrain myself or I will stop writing about Bible study and finish up writing about grace. Studying this kind of word takes a long time, but it is time well spent. Check in a concordance every verse in which the word occurs; look up each verse and write down one thing it says about grace. When you have done this, you should have a good grasp of what grace is. I warn you— it is a lot of things, and every one of them is beautiful!

Having looked into some of the words in the first two verses of Philippians, take another look at the verses and see the things I *didn't* mention. There are words so familiar we might not notice them. But dare we overlook them? The words we left out are these:

1. Christ
2. Jesus
3. God
4. Father
5. Lord

Every one of these words is important, and you should look at all of them. Remember that all we've done is examine two verses that didn't seem important at all in the first place. This gives you some idea of what Bible study holds for those who will work at it!

A Character Study

A third way to study the Bible is to look at a *character*. When Oliver Cromwell was having his portrait painted, he said that for it to be realistic he should be shown "warts and all." In fact, he said he would not pay the artist a farthing if he failed to do this. I think the Holy Spirit was given similar instructions from the Father when He was commissioned to "paint" the portraits of Biblical characters; most of them are shown to be real people with real problems, and in some instances they were shown to sink into deep sin. Yet God worked on them and did great things in their lives, which is why I believe all Christians should study Biblical characters. Through them we can see what God can do with ordinary people.

There's another reason, too. Some Christians seem to think God did remarkable things with people like Peter and Paul because they were abnormal men—saints stuck on plaster stands. But this is not true, and I believe the Word of God takes great pains to show us that fact. These people were weak, failing individuals as we are; nevertheless they had experiences that were superb. And so may we, for we have the same God.

To do a character study, first decide which figure interests you. Paul or David will rank high on everyone's list, but I suggest it is not wise to start with either. There is so much information about them, you might get lost in it. How about Stephen? He was a great man who made a tremendous impact and did it briefly.

Turn to *Stephen* in a concordance and read everything the Bible says about him. All the information on Stephen is found in the Book of Acts, most of it in chapters 6-8, so it isn't difficult to get the details together. When I studied this character, I noticed the following:

1. What he was, was irreproachable.
2. What he did was irrefutable.
3. What he said was irresistible.

You might look up the verses that give this information. Then

35

read Acts 6 and find one word used to describe Stephen. It occurs in connection with each of the following:

1. The Holy Spirit
2. Wisdom
3. Faith
4. Grace (translated *faith* in the *King James Version*)
5. Power

When you have found that word, you have found the secret of Stephen!

Then you might like to try Timothy, Silas, Mark, Jabez (yes, Jabez), Hannah, Mary, Ananias (both of them—be careful not to confuse them!), and when you're ready, do Peter! The approach is the same for all these characters, whether we know much about them or little. Find out everything the Bible says concerning them. Put it together in orderly form, perhaps by asking yourself questions like these:

1. Who was he (she)?
2. What did he do, say, think, desire?
3. Where did he do what he did?
4. Why was he the person he was?
5. Whom did he affect by his life?

There you have three ways to study your Bible. There are others, but I must stop now. After all, if I go on any longer, you won't have time for your Bible study—and that would be self-defeating!

CHAPTER 6

▼

LEARNING TO PRAY:
AN INTRODUCTION
by Stuart

Several years ago, after I preached in a church in Toronto, Canada, an elderly lady came up to me, took my hand, kissed it, and whispered, "I have prayed for you every day since you first preached in this church." Then she walked away before I had an opportunity even to ask her name. Old ladies rarely kiss my hand, but they may do it anytime if they tell me they pray for me daily! I love old ladies who pray!

"But I'm not an old lady," you say. True, some of the world's greatest praying people are old or infirm or both, but prayer is meant to be a vital part of *every* Christian's experience.

I think it is no coincidence that young people and active types have more difficulty with prayer than do older and more sedentary people. Activity-prone people tend to find quietness, meditation, and a "sweet hour of prayer" decidedly onerous and little more than a nice idea. The young and active tend to be self-sufficient, and this militates against prayer. But if youth, health, and vigor keep you from praying, then those qualities are not all they're cracked up to be.

Still, I admit I probably have more difficulty with prayer than with any other area of Christian experience. Because of this, I have given considerable thought and study to the subject, and I hope the results of this study are helpful to you. I suspect you may have trouble in this area, too, because most Christians I talk to about their problems put prayer high on the list of their failings and deficiencies.

I'm sure you've read of the great prayer warriors of the faith—like George Mueller, who ran that fantastic orphanage in Bristol, England, on the basis of prayer. He used to sit the kids down to eat and lead them in thanksgiving for the food, without there being a crumb on the table. But the food had a habit of arriving in response to prayer. He never asked donors for a penny, but lacked nothing for those children—and attributed it all to effective prayer.

No doubt you have heard of people like George Mueller, only to feel convicted and become discouraged. You may have thought, *How on earth can I pray like that and still make a living in today's society?* You may have decided as a result that prayer is for those who are "inclined that way"—and for you only when you feel like the small boy who said, "I pray when I want something and I think there is no other way of getting it."

So we need to start at the beginning and make sure we understand what prayer is. James Montgomery wrote,

Prayer is the soul's sincere desire,
Uttered or unexpressed,
The motion of a hidden fire that trembles in the breast.

That's beautiful, but what *is* it? Montgomery added that prayer is "the Christian's vital breath" and "native air." That's magnificent imagery, but perhaps we need more practical answers. I believe we've been too mystical and poetic about prayer; because it is a strange exercise of the human soul, we have tended to keep it delightfully vague, carefully couched in antiquated language and liberally peppered with clichés.

What is prayer? To me, it is *the talking part of a relationship.* We all know what it is to have a relationship with a spouse, child, parent, employer, or employee. We all know how necessary it is to have some verbal communication between participants in the relationship. One of the best ways to kill a marriage, a family, or a business is for the participants to stop talking to each other.

The Bible portrays the Christian experience as a relationship, among other things. We are Christ's friends (John 15:15), His servants (Colossians 3:24), and His bride (Romans 7:4). Prayer is the talking part of these relationships—friend talking to friend, servant to master, bride to spouse.

Why Pray?

If the aforementioned is a valid definition of prayer, it's only logical that the first reason to pray is *to develop our spiritual relationship*. Relationships that don't talk, don't grow.

"But isn't conversation a two-way street?" you might ask. "What's the talking part of the Lord in prayer?"

Strictly speaking, God does not converse in prayer. But He does talk through the Scriptures. Thus Bible reading and prayer go together; the former is the Lord talking to you, and the latter is your response. I am not saying you can pray only immediately after reading the Bible, but I believe the effectiveness of your prayer life is closely related to your depth in the Scriptures.

Similarly, the effectiveness of your Bible study can be largely determined by your prayer life. Conversations that have only one talker aren't conversations; they're monologues. The Lord's talking through Scripture to you and getting no response of prayer is not likely to build a relationship. Neither is your doing all the talking and ignoring the fact that He reserves the right to speak.

The second reason to pray is that *we have been told to* "Pray for them which . . . persecute you" (Matthew 5:44). "Pray to thy Father which is in secret" (Matthew 6:6). "Pray . . . the Lord of the harvest, that he will send forth labourers" (Matthew 9:38). "Watch and pray" (Matthew 26:41).

This brings a whole new dimension to prayer. Some people think they don't need to pray simply because they don't like it, just as they don't eat oysters because oysters are slippery. Whether they like to pray or not is irrelevant; they have been *told* to pray. Others feel too busy to pray and therefore feel quite happy not praying. But if they are too busy to do what they've been told to do, they must be too busy doing some things they have *not* been told to do!

Still others don't know how to pray—and never take the time

to find out. But not knowing how to pray is no excuse when God has given us so much information on the subject.

If we were free to pray only when we felt like it, we would probably do so only when something extraordinary happened—like seeing the number-three engine on our jumbo jet burst into flames over the polar ice cap, or discovering that our baby daughter has swallowed an unknown quantity of Mother's sleeping tablets. By all means, pray in these or similar situations; but prayer is much more than a last resort.

If we were free to pray only when we "had the time," we would probably never find the time. When did you last hear someone say, as he checked his watch at halftime during a football game, "Good, I have a few minutes to spare; I must do some praying"?

If we understand that prayer is commanded by our Lord, however, the whole picture changes. We discipline ourselves to pray when things are good *or* bad. We pray when we have a pious feeling and when we don't. Prayer becomes a discipline when we are busy doing something—or nothing. And learning to pray becomes a top priority.

It may seem strange that the Lord found it necessary to command us to pray. If we love Him, won't we automatically pray? Well, I find that even though I love the Lord and want to serve Him, there are so many distractions in my world, so many responsibilities in my vocation, so much *going on,* that I need a good, firm order once in a while to remind me.

This is a bit like loving your spouse. One might think that if a man loves his wife, for example, he will automatically love to do everything he should. It will be impossible for him to fail because he loves her so much. But he also loves his work, his football, his boat, and his kids; there are many demands on his time. Thus he faces the danger of taking his wife for granted and neglecting her, assuming all the time that "she knows I love her." He needs to discipline his time to express his love for her. So discipline is not the opposite of love; rather it is often the evidence of love.

The third reason to pray is *to follow the example of Christ.* If He needed to pray as much as He did, *we* certainly need to! On numerous occasions the Lord disciplined Himself to turn aside from everything else and pray. If *you* find it difficult to do that, how do you think *He* felt? In Matthew 14:23, for example, we read that He went away quietly to pray, but first had to send the people away. If there was one thing hard for the Lord to do, it was turning people away; He knew their needs as nobody else did.

He even stayed up all night to pray on at least one occasion (Luke 6:12). Missing a night's sleep is not easy, particularly when life is as full and busy as His was at that time. Prayer was a top priority with our Lord; nothing was to encroach on that priority.

Christ also made it clear to the disciples that He expected them to pray. He used the word *when*, not *if*, as He told them how to pray (Luke 11:2). It is clear that He means His followers to be people who, among other things, maintain a speaking relationship with God—through prayer.

When Should You Pray?
"OK," you may say. "Praying is a worthwhile endeavor. But do I have to stay up all night to do it? When *should* I pray, anyway?"

There are three "times" at which Christians should pray:

1. *Regularly.* Daniel was so organized in his praying that even when he was forbidden to pray on pain of being thrown to the lions, he went ahead anyway and prayed three times daily. While that doesn't mean you have to pray "morning, noon, and night," it wouldn't be a bad idea. I suggest you plan a time of prayer—one that is right for you—into your regular schedule the way you plan eating and sleeping.

Your regular prayer should include regular attendance at church services where you can pray during the "pastoral prayer" (if your worship service offers one). In the church I pastor, we lay heavy emphasis on the time of prayer in all our services. When the pastor prays in the service, that is not the time to think about your finances or whether you left the car's lights on; you should pray along with him.

41

For the same reasons, you should also form the habit of joining your fellow church members when they meet to pray. It's a sad commentary on our attitude toward prayer that most church prayer meetings are poorly attended.

You should pray regularly at mealtimes, too. Even when you eat away from home you can bow your head in thanksgiving and witness—nothing ostentatious, but nothing to be ashamed of either. Don't pretend to rub the nonexistent sleep out of your eyes, but don't kneel on your napkin beside the table and boom out a prayer for the benefit of bemused diners nearby. When Jill first bowed her head to pray in a restaurant, she opened her eyes to find an old woman looking anxiously at her and saying, "Here's an aspirin. Have you got a headache, Luv?"

You should also try to have some regular prayer with your family if possible. They might not like the idea at first, but it's amazing how they can grow into it. We have not done all we should with our kids in this matter, but what we've done has been a delight.

Doubtless there are other times when you can pray regularly, but I leave it to you to find them.

2. *Spontaneously.* Nehemiah (see the Old Testament book named for him) did this beautifully. As the royal cupbearer, he was not allowed to look unhappy in the king's presence. One day he received some bad news from home and naturally was upset. He forgot to put on his stage smile, and the king demanded to know why he was looking sad. That spelled trouble for Nehemiah, and he admitted to being "sore afraid"—but he took a deep breath and "prayed to the God of heaven" (Nehemiah 2:4).

That doesn't mean he said to the king, "Every knee bowed, every eye closed. . . ." It means he flashed a very quick prayer to Heaven between heartbeats—something like, "Help!"

That is what I call spontaneous praying. You will need to do it often when you are faced with danger or decision. The more you practice prayer, the more of a reflex action spontaneous prayer will become.

3. *Continually.* "Pray without ceasing" (I Thessalonians 5:17) can raise some eyebrows. Those who think praying is done only

in church will have to move into church permanently to pray without ceasing. Those who feel you must close your eyes and bend your knees to pray will become a terrible hazard when driving in that position on the freeway. Obviously this is not what the Bible has in mind.

Prayer is not only a definite act, but it is also a continual attitude. The thought behind continual prayer is not that your life should be spent in the act of prayer, but that your spirit should live in an attitude of prayer. It is an attitude of humble thanksgiving, reverent awe, childlike dependence, and expectant faith. It is an attitude that swiftly and easily at the slightest sign of necessity slips into the act of prayer.

This attitude is also of great practical help. Often I drive with the radio on to keep me awake; the information coming over the airwaves frequently stirs me to pray as I drive. As I run my morning mile, I run in an attitude of prayer as well. On the first lap I pray for the family, on the second for the church, and on the third for outside activities. And on the fourth lap? I pray, "Lord, give me breath for this unfinished task!"

Thus we have some long answers to the short questions, "What is prayer?" and "Why should we pray?" and "When should we pray?" I hope the answers are stimulating and challenging enough to make you want to go further in the adventure of prayer.

CHAPTER 7

▼

LEARNING TO PRAY: GETTING TO KNOW GOD

by Stuart

Many hang-ups about prayer must be sorted out before some people will get around to praying. A few Christians get the idea from some of us preachers that God understands only "olde fashionede Englyshe," and that unless they talk like King James, God will not hear them. This naturally causes problems, because many people get into tongue-twisting difficulties with *wilt, wert, thee,* and *thou*—not to mention having heart attacks at having to contemplate *lookedst* and *lettest.*

At the risk of offending friends who think antiquated terminology is the only valid expression of reverence, let me say definitely that prayer should be natural. So if thou naturally talkest like this, thou shouldest pray like this; but if thou dost not, thou dost not have to pray like this.

Nevertheless, all who really approach God in prayer must have a sense of reverence. That demands standards of decorum and good taste that rule out silliness, looseness, and glibness. If you talk to a person of some standing whom you deeply respect, you do so in a manner that expresses that respect.

What Should We Pray?
If the "style" of prayer is natural, what is the content? What should we say as we get to know God through this speaking relationship?

The following acrostic provides an outline:

P stands for *Praise*
R stands for *Repentance*
A stands for *Asking*
Y stands for *Yourself*

Praying includes praising God. Prayer is not simply the presentation of a celestial shopping list. It is to include worshiping God, acknowledging Him and the wonders of His goodness and the greatness of His love.

We must never forget that the greatest thing about being a human being—as opposed to being a chimpanzee or a carrot—is that we can know God and glorify Him. To glorify Him means to respond to Him in such a way that He can be seen in our attitudes toward Him. The ways we think about Him, respond to Him, obey Him, and thank Him are all part of glorifying Him. When we pray in praise, we do one of the most wonderful things humans can: glorifying Him in our attitudes and putting this into words. For me, one of the best ways is to read my Bible and, upon discovering something new about God or being reminded of something I'd forgotten about His character, to thank Him for being the kind of Person He is and for doing the things He does.

Here's an example. Before I began to write this chapter, I turned to my Bible and read Isaiah 48. In this chapter, many things are said about God. I didn't have time to list them, but I did bow my head and meditate on what it means that *He is.* After thinking about these things and thanking Him for them, I read verse 18: "Then had thy peace been as a river. . . ." Guess what hymn I started humming in praise? I was able to praise the Lord at my typewriter!

You will get material for praise not only from Scripture, but also from another beautiful part of His revelation—nature. A quiet walk on a cool morning of a fresh, new day can make your spirit rejoice. Remember that your praise should be directed to the One who made the day. You may find help in singing quietly,

▼

When morning gilds the skies,
My heart awaking cries,
May Jesus Christ be praised.

There is another area in which you should be stimulated to praise: answered prayer and blessings received. Saying "thank You" is common courtesy sometimes overlooked in our dealings with God. Remember how Jesus healed ten lepers, and 90 percent didn't say "thank You" (Luke 17:12-19)? That is a sad statistic, and I fear it is repeated in our day. Try being thankful regularly.

Second, *prayer includes repentance*. When our children were small and we were trying to teach them to pray, we had three kinds of prayer: "Please prayers," "Thank-You prayers," and "Sorry prayers." It will come as no surprise that we had no problem getting the first, a slight problem getting the second, and major problems getting the third. The children had the hardest time thinking of something for which to be sorry, and when they eventually thought of it (usually with our help), saying "sorry" did not come easily.

I'm afraid this is a problem which troubles many adults as well as kids. It really is difficult for us to admit we have done something wrong, and even more difficult for us to say we are sorry about it. But whether it is difficult or not is beside the point. The Scriptures insist that we "confess our sins" and further promise that if we do, God will "forgive us our sins, and . . . cleanse us from all unrighteousness" (I John 1:9).

If a person goes on sinning, never admits it, and never confesses, it is only a matter of time until he will have no fellowship with the Lord. But if he searches his own life carefully, exposes his sins and failings, and is genuinely concerned about them, he will experience not only the joy of cleansing, but also the freshness of renewed fellowship.

Allow me to make some suggestions about confession and repentance. I have heard people pray at mealtimes and conclude with a phrase like, "and forgive us our many sins." This is good as far as it goes. It shows that the person is conscious of sin, is

47

willing to deal with it, and wants forgiveness and cleansing. But the prayer needs to be more specific. I find the words of "The General Confession" very helpful: "We have left undone those things which we ought to have done: And we have done those things which we ought not to have done; and there is no health in us."

Notice three things: First, the failure to do expected things; second, the doing of forbidden things; third, the sense of personal unworthiness in the sight of God. These are necessary ingredients in prayer of this nature. But in our private and personal prayers we need to get more specific. Ask yourself, "What exactly did I do that I was told not to do? Did I sin with my eyes, my lips, my mind, my attitude? What exactly did I not do that the Lord expected me to do? Did I fail to love, to speak, to help, to give, to worship?"

When you have some answers to questions like these, you are ready for confession and repentance. Of course, one of the by-products of repentance is that if you have to be repentant about the same thing often enough, you might get so embarrassed about it that you are motivated to turn from it and forsake it. Read Psalm 51 if you want an example of a man praying a prayer of repentance and confession.

Third, *praying includes asking.* I realize I have put third what many people put first. And I have found it necessary to keep a tight rein on my praying lest I do the same thing. But if praise is equivalent to "thank you" and repentance is equivalent to "sorry," then asking is like saying "please." To be interested only in please, forgetful about thank you and never sorry is to be extremely immature.

There is no doubt that God wants us to ask Him for things. Jesus said, "Ask, and it shall be given you; seek, and ye shall find; knock, and it shall be opened unto you" (Matthew 7:7).

But for what kinds of things can we ask? A good answer is found in the Lord's Prayer. Look at what Christ taught us to ask for in Matthew 6:

1. That God's name be honored and respected (v. 9).

2. That God's Kingdom be completed (v. 10).
3. That God's will be implemented (v. 10).

Note that your asking prayers should be motivated by these three great desires. This automatically rules out praying something like, "Lord, I want a Cadillac—and You said, 'Ask and you shall receive.' So I'm going to extend my garage immediately in faith." That kind of prayer seems to have in mind the name, Kingdom, and will of the person praying—not those of the Lord. You don't need to get any hang-ups about this, constantly trying to figure out whose will you have in mind at any one point—just as long as you don't think you can take off in any old direction and ask for anything that comes into your mind. If your heart is set on God's honor and will and Kingdom, then His Spirit will lead you into the right prayer channels.

Now let's be more specific. The Lord's Prayer goes on to talk about your needing to ask concerning

4. Physical needs: daily bread (v. 11)
5. Social needs: forgiving and being forgiven (v. 12)
6. Spiritual needs: temptation and deliverance (v. 13).

Those three areas of need are vast—and give us the green light to ask about things that are physical and social as well as spiritual.

But there is another lesson to be learned from the Lord's Prayer. Read it to yourself and see how many times the words *I, me,* or *mine* occur. Surprised to discover that none of them appears at all? This is staggering when you think of the way we pray! When you ask in prayer, you should be concerned with the name, Kingdom, and will of God as they relate to *others*.

Fourth, *praying includes yourself.* Praying for yourself is not wrong. The Lord did it in the Garden of Gethsemane, though He prayed that His Father's will, not His own, would be done. David prayed for himself, but notice in Psalm 51 that his purpose was that "sinners shall be converted" (v. 13) and God would be worshiped (v. 19).

I feel we'll have no difficulty praying for ourselves correctly if we remember that "Y" is the *last* letter in "P.R.A.Y." Problems occur only when we get "Y" up front. In fact, sometimes our praying is so out of order that we do it this way:

Y for *Yourself*
A for *Asking*
R for *Repentance*
P for *Praise*

And that's not praying—it's "yarping"!

CHAPTER 8

▼

SHOWING LOVE
FOR THE CHURCH

by Stuart

The church in which I was brought up had no buildings, no minister, and practically no congregation! For a while we met in the front room of my parents' home; later we used the rear offices of a soda pop factory. Today, on the other hand, I am the senior pastor of a church with 13 on its pastoral staff, a magnificent facility on 34 acres, and a weekly attendance of about 6,000.

In between these two experiences I have met with believers on every continent in practically every kind of facility imaginable—from beautful cathedrals with soaring arches to mud huts with sagging palm leaf roofs. Some of the congregations dripped diamonds; others barely wore clothes. In some of the churches people grumbled because they had to walk from the back of the parking lot; in others people picked thorns from their bare feet as I preached.

That's how I've learned that the Church is not the building—it's the people. When Christ said He would build His Church (Matthew 16:18), He was referring to those who would become His disciples and band together to be His people in discernible, distinctive ways.

This is not adequately understood. How often we say things like, "What church do you go to?" "Is there a gymnasium in your church?" Clearly we need facilities, but only to facilitate the Church being the Church! When buildings take the place of people or become an end in themselves, they have diverted our attention from being the Church—and turned us into just another group of people who meet in a building.

Then what is special about this group of people? The answer is that they have a special relationship with a special Person called Jesus Christ. This relationship is based on their recognition of their own sinfulness—which immediately sets them apart from most other groups—and the belief that only Christ through His death and resurrection can forgive them and provide reconciliation to God. Accordingly they are—or should be—characterized by gratitude to Him, which they express through unique activities. These activities include *fellowship, worship, stewardship,* and *discipleship.*

Fellowship

It is very difficult to have fellowship with yourself! I know some people are loners and others social butterflies, but I'm not talking about the fact that some people enjoy their own company more than that of others. I'm referring to the fact that Christians need to be characterized by *sharing* in order to express their love for the Lord. That's what Jesus meant when He said, "I tell you the truth, whatever you did for one of the least of these brothers of mine, you did for me" (Matthew 25:40, NIV).

The flip side of fellowship is that Christians need each other for the help and encouragement required for the rough road ahead. Joys and sorrows need to be shared; Christians must learn to "Rejoice with those who rejoice; mourn with those who mourn" (Romans 12:15, NIV).

Worship

It is possible, of course, to worship on your own. In fact, it's necessary for the Christian to develop a private devotional life. But Christians have traditionally met for corporate worship, too.

Worshiping together became one of the trademarks of the Church, which began in Jerusalem within a couple of months after Christ's ascension. There believers met regularly and "devoted themselves to the apostles' teaching and to the fellowship, to the breaking of bread and to prayer" (Acts 2:42, NIV). This kind of worship flowed quite naturally from established patterns of synagogue and temple worship with which the Jewish converts were familiar. When Paul and other missionaries began to reach the Gentile world, they also taught the necessity of gathering together to express love for the Lord and for each other.

As I have worshiped with God's people across the globe, I've been thrilled to see the many ways in which different people can express their understanding of God's worth (remember, worship means an expression of *God's worth*). I have sat cross-legged on the hard floors of little huts in Bangladesh, where old men converted from Islam spent endless hours talking about their discoveries in God's Word. When they paused to express their appreciation to Him, their long prayers were unintelligible to me; but their love for the Lord knew no barriers of language or culture.

In Africa I have sung and swayed to the beat of drums and hollowed-out gourds as believers there sang praises to their Savior long into the night. Their enthusiasm was as infectious as their rhythms. There was something uniquely African about the way they did things, yet there was something uniquely Christian about their objective to honor the Lord. Worship takes so many forms and includes so many things—but it always results in God being glorified and the worshipers being helped, blessed, refreshed, challenged, and encouraged.

Stewardship
When we think of stewardship we tend to think of fund raising. This is unfortunate, because stewardship is something else entirely.

In New Testament times a steward looked after the assets and resources of another person. For instance, when a businessman went on a journey he would leave his affairs in the care of a steward. When the master returned, the steward would be required to give an account of his activities (Luke 12:42). This practice was applied by the Lord Jesus and the apostles to the kind of lives Christians should live. Christians, of all people, ought to realize that the things they possess are not really theirs at all. They agree with the Psalmist that "the earth is the Lord's, and everything in it" (Psalm 24:1, NIV).

Stewardship, therefore, is an attitude which motivates Christians to use their resources, financial and otherwise, in light of the fact that they really belong to God; we are simply handling these resources for Him. Christians should give as unto the Lord, channeling their funds in a way that will finance the Lord's work in their immediate fellowship and even worldwide.

Stewardship is more than a matter of money, though; Christians also donate time, energy, and skills to the Lord in their everyday work and in specific acts of service and charity. The latter often need to be coordinated and supported, a task the Church can well perform. Blessed indeed is the Christian who delights in acts of service and sacrifice which demonstrate devotion to the Lord—and to the Church's task of showing God's love in ways that cause people to glorify Him.

Discipleship

The Lord Jesus made it clear that He was committed to making disciples, and that His disciples should in turn become disciple makers themselves. The first thing He did in His public ministry was to collect His disciples, and the last thing He did before leaving was to commission them to disciple the nations.

A disciple is not someone who wears a long, white bathrobe and a pair of sandals. He or she is a person who follows Christ while wearing a three-piece suit, an apron, or whatever his or her vocation requires. One young lady in a premembership class in our church, for example, introduced herself as "a disciple of Jesus Christ skillfully disguised as a machine operator."

The essence of discipleship is ordinary people in ordinary walks of life refusing to be pressed into the mold of the society around them; instead they take seriously the teachings and promises of Christ and live according to them. Rather than being blown about by the prevailing winds of philosophy, they choose to be different when the prevailing mood contradicts the truth proclaimed by Christ.

An example: There is a widely accepted sexual moral code which disciples of Jesus Christ must declare to be totally unacceptable. This is not because they are some kind of eunuchs who have lost all sexual feeling and desire. It is because they regard generally accepted mores as wrong—and the widely rejected teachings of Christ on the subject to be right! Therefore they choose to follow Him.

When men and women become followers of Christ, they naturally need to learn many new things—and unlearn a lot of old ones. The process of learning and unlearning is an integral part of being a disciple, and the best place to learn is in a church where all kinds of disciples are going through the same experience. Some prefer to think of discipleship as a relationship between two people; one is the discipler, the other the disciple. This has proven to be a valuable approach for countless thousands of Christians, but it should be pointed out that Jesus did not operate "one on one." He discipled about 12 at a time. It would seem advisable for us to go the same route, since limiting ourselves to "one on one" can result in transmitting personal prejudices and quirks from discipler to disciple. The interaction of a group can act as a safeguard and offers broader opportunity for support and discovery.

The Church, then, is a community of people gathered in the name of the Lord Jesus. This community offers itself individually and collectively to Him, and in so doing glorifies Him—and grows. But there is one unfortunate problem with churches; they are made up entirely and exclusively of sinners! So if you're looking for a perfect church, you'll have a terrible time finding one. And if you find one, be sure not to join it. After all, you'd ruin it!

CHAPTER 9

▼

LEARNING OBEDIENCE
by Jill

If you love me, you will obey what I command (John 14:15, NIV).

Why did Jesus say that to His disciples? What do love and obedience have to do with each other?

I believe love and obedience are like marriage partners. You might say they produce lively offspring called joy, peace, and power.

Obedience and Joy

I can well remember the joy I felt when my children began to obey me of their own free wills. Greater joy lay ahead when, returning from a trip, I found they had been obedient without having me around to monitor their progress! They were saying, in effect, "When you love someone, you want to please him or her. So it's really quite easy to do what you've told us to do." Obeying loved ones brings pleasure to our hearts *and* theirs.

We often begin the Christian life obeying because we're told that Christians *should* be obedient. That's hard at first, because being obedient frequently means doing things we really don't want to do! Bad habits have to be broken, apologies made, letters or phone calls initiated to mend broken relationships. There can be a lot to undo when one has spent years living selfishly.

Being obedient because we *should* be is fine—at the beginning. It breaks the cycle of selfishness. But it's not the highest and best motive. Even though God is happy to start there with us, He is not willing to leave us living the Christian life at that low level. He wants us to grow into more mature modes of behavior.

We know we are developing as Christians when we find ourselves being obedient not because we *should* be, but because we *want* to be. This happens as we come to know God more thoroughly. After all, to know Him is to love Him, and to love Him is to obey Him. This *glad* obedience brings delight to the heart of God, and finds its happiness reflected in our own souls.

Jesus Christ furnishes us with the grand example of this delighted obedience. It is written of Him:

> Then said he, Lo, I come to do thy will, O God (Hebrews 10:9).

> Looking unto Jesus the author and finisher of our faith; who for the joy that was set before him endured the cross, despising the shame, and is set down at the right hand of the throne of God (Hebrews 12:2).

> My meat is to do the will of him that sent me, and to finish his work (John 4:34).

> If a man love me, he will keep my words: and my Father will love him, and we will come unto him, and make our abode with him. But that the world may know that I love the Father; and as the Father gave me commandment, even so I do (John 14:23, 31).

> I have glorified thee on the earth: I have finished the work which thou gavest me to do (John 17:4).

There is a totally unique joy that comes through doing God's will. But first we have to find out what He wants us to do! By studying His Word and noting His commands therein, we come to understand what He wants for us. God's commands are His rules, and rules are to be obeyed.

Obedience and Peace

Obedience produces peace as well as joy. There is a certain tranquillity about being obedient; to know in your heart that you have done the right thing rather than the convenient, profitable, or selfish thing brings an order and stillness into our souls. It is the tranquillity only obedient children know.

For example, it is hard to sleep well when you are being willfully disobedient. Shortly after becoming a Christian I began to date a non-Christian. I had read the verse that says, "Be ye not unequally yoked together with unbelievers: for what fellowship hath righteousness with unrighteousness? and what communion hath light with darkness?" (II Corinthians 6:14). I understood that a romantic commitment to a nonbeliever when I had a choice in the matter was sheer disobedience, but I tried hard to rationalize my behavior. *Perhaps I'll win him to Christ,* I told myself. *How would he hear the Gospel if I don't tell him?* Perhaps I even tried to persuade myself that God didn't really mean what He said to the apostle Paul!

Let me tell you, I did not sleep well in those days! Even my waking hours were interrupted with disturbing thoughts. I had no tranquillity until I decided to be obedient. Then I slept!

I am not saying that if you can't sleep it's because you are disobeying God. But there's a good chance that a guilty conscience will drive sleep far from you—and trouble your waking hours. As Scripture indicates: "Great peace have they which love thy law: and nothing shall offend them" (Psalm 119:165).

Obedience and Power

Obedience is also the mother of power. As you obey, you find the power to do so keeps up with you! It does not come before or linger after. The power of God, made available to the obedient Christian, keeps in step with our right actions. It is there for us to appropriate for the doing of the life of love.

When I returned to college after receiving Christ, I became aware of a Biblical command that I was disobeying. Many verses instructed me to tell people about Christ; there were no exceptions. I knew many of my friends had not rejected Christ, but had never had a chance to receive Him. I had reneged on my responsibility because I didn't want to risk losing those who mattered most to me.

"Lord," I protested, "I don't have the power to do this. If You give me the power first, then I'll tell them."

"You tell them first," He seemed to reply, "and then I'll give you the power as you go through with it!"

There was that principle again. Our obedient actions allow His Spirit to enable us to carry through our good intentions. God has promised as much:

> With men this is impossible; but with God all things are possible (Matthew 19:26).

> And Jesus came and spake unto them, saying, All power is given unto me in heaven and in earth. Go ye therefore, and teach all nations, baptizing them in the name of the Father, and of the Son, and of the Holy Ghost: Teaching them to observe all things whatsoever I have commanded you: and, lo, I am with you alway, even unto the end of the world (Matthew 28:18-20).

> My grace is sufficient for thee: for my strength is made perfect in weakness. Most gladly therefore will I rather glory in my infirmities, that the power of Christ may rest upon me (II Corinthians 12:9, 10).

Obedience, Love, and Happiness

I suppose it all comes down to loving God. Joy, peace, and power are produced when we recognize our role in the fruit-producing part of that relationship. Our role is to obey. To love God in the truest sense means to be primarily concerned with

His will and His feelings—irrespective of the cost to oneself. It is not first a matter of our emotions, but of concern to find and do the truth. The first question obedience asks love should be, "What is the right thing to do?" Once the answer has been determined, then we must do it no matter what our feelings—since our feelings might well be telling us to do the opposite! As we *do* the truth because of our loving concern for God, He will provide the strength. "Faithful is he that calleth you, who also will do it" (I Thessalonians 5:24).

Part of the power to "continue continuing" will be a peace of mind that passes understanding—which will release energy formerly used to strive against God! Joy follows, chasing down our worried spirits, filling us to overflowing with the warm knowledge that we are pleasing God.

In the end, where is happiness? In living the obedient Christian life!

CHAPTER 10

▼

TALKING ABOUT FAITH: WHO NEEDS IT?

by Stuart

Just mention the word *witnessing* and some people run for their Bibles and booklets—while others run for cover! The whole business of talking about one's faith really gets to people in the Christian community. If "witnessing" is not adequately understood, it can indeed be scary.

A friend of mine tells a magnificent story of his first attempts at witnessing. He was punched in the nose by a small boy and bitten on the leg by a large dog in no time at all! Needless to say, his enthusiasm ebbed as his blood flowed.

The word *witness* is used in various ways in Scripture. Leviticus 5:1 states that if a person is under oath to be a witness and does not testify truthfully, he will be held responsible. Obviously this kind of witnessing has to do with courts of law where people are required to explain what they have seen and heard. Genesis 31 tells the story of those two rascals, Laban and Jacob, who had spent years sharpening their wits on each other. Eventually they came to some agreement and built a big heap of stones as a "witness" to that agreement. In this sense the word means to give visible evidence of an invisible experience.

In the New Testament there is an interesting aspect to the word *witness*. The Greek word for "witness" is *martus*; you don't have to know much Greek or English to see the connection between *martus* and *martyr*. In the gory days of the early church, to be a witness was almost a guarantee you would be a martyr.

If we put these ideas together, we see that a witness is *someone who by explanation and demonstration gives audible and visible evidence of what he or she has seen and heard, without being deterred by the consequences.* That's my definition, for what it's worth. We should refine that definition further by noting that Christians have a particular *subject* in mind when they think of sharing their experiences and convictions: their knowledge of Christ, from both the theoretical and practical points of view. So a Christian witness is one who, in a variety of ways, communicates the truth as it is to be found in Christ.

I have labored over that definition because I find that many people have seen or experienced only one method of witnessing—and sometimes they have had a bad experience and decided never to witness again. I'm glad my friend who got beaten and bitten did not take this attitude, because he is now one of the most effective missionaries I know in the Spanish-speaking world. He discovered that some approaches to giving "audible and visible evidence" were not his line at all. But he didn't quit; he found other ways.

You may have tried going door to door with the Four Spiritual Laws and loved it, but your partner curled up and died every time you rang a doorbell. You were praying, "Lord, give me the words to speak," and she was praying, "Lord, I hope they're not at home."

We can see that one method of witnessing may appeal to one person, and other methods to another. We must not lock people into any one system of doing it, nor must we allow them to overlook the necessity of their having an effective approach to witnessing.

Why Witness?

Why is it important that Christians witness? Why can't the preachers get on with it while the other folks work to pay them for doing it?

First, *Christ insisted that we should witness.* Speaking from the Mount of Olives immediately before He ascended to Heaven, the Lord Jesus said, "Ye shall be witnesses unto me" (Acts 1:8).

He said many other things at that point which help us to grasp the "how" and "where" of what He had in mind, but right now let's concentrate on that brief statement.

It is important to note that the Lord did not say, "Wouldn't it be lovely if we could share a little of what we have learned with those who haven't had a chance to learn?" And He didn't say, "Hands up, all those who feel like doing a little witnessing!" No, His approach was straight to the point: "You shall be witnesses."

The disciples got the message. It was unavoidable, and it should not be overlooked today. The question is not whether you will *be* a witness; the point is that if you are a Christian, you *are* a witness. The only options open to you are to be "good, bad, or indifferent."

Or to put it another way, once a woman is married, she doesn't decide whether or not to be a wife. She rejected that option the moment she took her vows. Her only remaining options are whether or not to be a *good* wife!

It must be admitted that the Lord was talking to His select group of disciples when He gave these instructions. Thus some people today believe these words were applicable only to those who heard them. But the Lord taught His original disciples so they might teach others until the whole world knew about Him. Therefore these things do apply to us today. He still says, "You shall be witnesses."

Second, *Christ did a lot of it Himself.* The variety of our Lord's ministry is one of its most beautiful characteristics. Sometimes He spoke to crowds, sometimes to individuals. A read through the Gospels will show the many personal conversations Jesus had; He did a lot of "personal evangelism." If Jesus is our example, isn't His witnessing an example, too?

Third, *God ordained that we should be witnesses.* "All this is from God, who reconciled us to himself through Christ and gave us the ministry of reconciliation: that God was reconciling the world to himself in Christ, not counting men's sins against them. And he has committed to us the message of reconciliation" (II Corinthians 5:18, 19, NIV).

If you have been reconciled to God (restored to harmony with Him through Christ) you have been given a ministry of reconciliation (helping others to be restored to harmony with Him). On the one hand you were given reconciliation and, on the other, a ministry. Many people do not figure that God works this way, but He does. He gives blessings in order to make the blessed become the means of blessing. What He puts in, He expects to pop out. With God, input leads to output. You can't be reconciled to God without being recruited!

That being the case, the world must be teeming with people in the reconciliation business. Unfortunately, many of them don't know they are in it—or know and wish they didn't.

Fourth, *the world needs us to be witnesses.* I didn't say the world *wants* us to be witnesses, but it certainly needs us! "Let him know, that he which converteth the sinner from the error of his way, shall save a soul from death, and shall hide a multitude of sins" (James 5:20). Three things are mentioned in this verse that one human being can do for another:

a. *He can convert him from the error of his way.* Some people know they are living in error, but many don't. Think of it: some with whom you rub shoulders every day are heading in the wrong direction with every step they take. They are building their lives on a false foundation, living lifestyles based on false philosophy, filling their hearts with false hope. They are in error, in danger of arriving at the wrong destination and not knowing it until they get there. Their whole lives may be devoted to meaningless causes, while important issues are never considered.

But you can change all that! Through an effective witness to Christ, you can lead that person from error to truth.

b. *He can save his soul from death.* If you jump into the river and pull someone out, you'll be a hero. Yet you will have saved someone from death only to have him or her die later. Don't misunderstand; if you get the chance, do it! But if you realize that saving someone physically is little more than postponing the inevitable, how about considering saving somebody's soul? If you want to be a real hero, do something more than postpone the inevitable—change that person's whole eternal destiny through an effective witness used by the Holy Spirit.

c. *He can hide a multitude of his sins.* God doesn't have a failing memory. He doesn't overlook sin, either. What's more, He is eternal, so that what we call the past is the present to Him, and what hasn't happened yet is in the now with Him. If this is confusing, it is also sobering—because it means the considerable mind of God is fully aware of all that has gone by in our lives. And all that has gone past includes an awful lot of sins—a multitude of them.

This is serious beyond description, because people are responsible beings who must stand before God and give an answer for their sins. There can be no evasion, no postponement, no tricky defense lawyer—just each person and God and a multitude of sins. But because of Christ, we can say, "As far as the east is from the west, so far hath he removed our transgressions from us" (Psalm 103:12). That's all because Christ's sacrifice for sin is applicable to all who come to Him in repentance and faith.

You can tell people about that by being a witness. You can tell people there is forgiveness through the grace of God. You can help hide a multitude of sins.

I should emphasize that God does the converting, saving, and hiding. We are the means through which the message is spread. Can you think of a greater need in our world than the need for the saving, restoring, enriching message of Christ to be given to more and more people? I can't!

Who Cares?

Just as we can watch a TV documentary about famine in Ethiopia, only to switch off the set and pop a frozen pizza in the microwave oven, we can understand all the reasons why Christians should witness, believe them thoroughly, get all convicted and convinced—and never do a thing about it.

At first glance this would appear to be nothing more than callous indifference. But I think there's more to it. A sense of helplessness and hopelessness can pervade the famine watchers and silent witnesses; they feel the little they could do would make no difference. Thus they turn away and try to forget what they know of the need.

I am sure that if more people were shown exactly what to do, they would lose their helpless, hopeless feelings—and get moving. So let me explain what you need to do.

You need to get some concern. That's great, isn't it? You didn't need someone to tell you that. Still, there is no way of avoiding this point; if you are not concerned about others' spiritual condition, you will do nothing to alter it. The problem, as I see it, is that many people are guilty because of their lack of concern—but don't know how to get some! What are the reasons for this unconcern?

1. *There are spiritual reasons for a lack of concern.* When the Holy Spirit is really working in your life, He motivates in special ways. He gives you a love for things you used to dislike, and a distaste for things you used to enjoy immensely. He also begins to deal with inbred selfishness and help you see the conditions of those around you.

But you can stop Him from doing this work in your life. You can "grieve" Him and "quench" Him. You may find yourself rebelling against His prompting. You may even allow your reaction to His work to become stronger than His leading. Then you're in trouble, for you are hindering His work, quenching His motivation and grieving Him.

What can you do about this problem? Recognize it when it happens, admit it to yourself, and confess it to the Lord. Tell Him, "Lord, I'm just being selfish. I know from Your prompting in my heart that I should be thinking about the needs of frightened, discouraged Mrs. Finkelschnitzel who is in the hospital. I know You are bringing her to my mind, and I know I could take her a word of comfort from Scripture. But to do that I would have to miss my hair appointment, and . . ."

That is being honest, but it isn't enough. So decide whether you are going to say, ". . . and, Lord, I won't quench Your Spirit; I won't grieve You. I'll cancel the appointment. I'll go and see her for Your sake—and I'll wear a wig!"

2. *There are theological reasons for a lack of concern.* Anyone

who has done any Bible study at all is aware that such words as *hell, condemned, perish,* and *wrath* are found there in rather large quantities. But many "Bible-believing Christians" don't really believe the Bible when what it says is so challenging and sobering.

Herein lies the problem. Believers who don't really believe what they profess to believe need to reevaluate their theological positions and have the courage to abide by the implications. In other words, if you believe there is a hell and people are perishing under the wrath of God, you must let that belief move you to concern and action. If, on the other hand, you do not accept the reality of these things, feel perfectly free to be unconcerned about the spiritual well-being of others.

Please get your theology cleared up at this point. Are people lost or aren't they? Is there a hell or not? Do people face the wrath of God or don't they? If your answers are in the affirmative, let your theology get into your bloodstream and take it to its conclusion. Then concern will come.

General William Booth, founder of the Salvation Army, could never be accused of mincing words or doing things half-heartedly. He believed that if he could hold each of his officers over hell for a few minutes, he would have no trouble keeping each one motivated about being a witness to Christ.

3. *There are practical reasons for lack of concern.* If you care about witnessing, you will have to stand up and be counted—which could bring some abuse. Years ago I was praying with one of my children at bedtime, and I asked him if he had any problems we should pray about. He couldn't think of any, though I could think of a number! Rather unwisely, I pressed the point and asked, "Don't you have any problems at school?"

"No," he replied firmly.

"Don't the kids give you a hard time because you're a Christian?"

Again the answer was no.

Thinking back to my own traumatic school days, I said, "But kids *always* give you a hard time if you let them know you're a Christian."

His reply was frank beyond belief: "All the more reason you don't let them know!" With that, quite happily, he turned over to sleep.

With the refreshing candor of the very young, he had put into words the practical reasons why many Christians don't witness. They don't want to take the consequences. In all fairness to my son, I must explain that he came to see things differently and went on to be used by God in numerous lives at school.

Another practical problem is that some people are willing, but feel unable. They fear that if they open their mouths, they'll insert their feet. This feeling is understandable, but always remember that God does not expect you to share what you don't know. He expects you to share what you *do* know. If you are primarily worried about how you will look in a witnessing encounter, your concern for your image outweighs your concern for those who really need the Lord.

Thus, if you lack concern for those who don't know Christ, try the following:

1. Find out whether selfishness is controlling your actions so much that the Holy Spirit can't work in you. Recognize this as wrong, confess it, and ask the Holy Spirit to give you His concern for those who need the Lord.

2. Check your theology, especially the parts relating to each person's condition before God. Is your behavior consistent with your belief? If not, ask God to help you have the courage to be consistent.

3. List all the hang-ups you have about witnessing. Pray about each one and begin to see them in the light of what God has told you to do.

4. *Continue* to do these things—because if you don't, you'll find other concerns taking the place of this one.

CHAPTER 11

▼

TALKING ABOUT FAITH: YOU CAN DO IT!

by Stuart

Once you're concerned enough to share your faith, what do you do? How do you go about it? Here are some basics.

Making Contact

First, you'll need to make some contacts with non-Christians. Scripture uses numerous contact makers to illustrate the activity of witnesses; at different times we are called *fishermen, ambassadors, reapers,* and *watchmen.* Fishermen have to make contact with fish; ambassadors have to present themselves at the court of the nation to which they are sent; reapers must go where the oats are; and watchmen have to stay where the action is.

The whole business of making contact is difficult for many people—so difficult, in fact, that they refuse to do it. Then they have to defend their position by putting the blame on the other party. Some Christians seem to think people do not find Christ because they don't go to church. But I think the real reason is because the Church doesn't go to them. Fishermen don't sit at home grumbling because the fish aren't knocking at the door, asking to be caught. Reapers don't account for their lack of harvest by blaming the oats for not jumping into the barn. And the U.S. ambassador to England certainly doesn't sit in his apartment and say, "If the Queen wants me to be an ambassador to her country, she'd better come to Washington and get me." The responsibility to make contact rests on the witness, fisherman, or whatever you want to call him.

71

It is a rare person who has no contacts. Even lonely old ladies see the mailman occasionally. Most of us rub shoulders with hundreds of people. Start thinking about all those people you know. Has it ever occurred to you that you could reasonably expect to be a witness to them? It might help you to make a list of all the people with whom you have any kind of contact. Then start to pray for them, asking God to give you a chance to talk to them sometime.

The people at the top of your list will probably be relatives, friends, and workmates—those you see on a regular basis. They may know you only as husband, boss, son, or tennis partner, but they also need to know you as a Christian. This will require some words on your part, though actions may indeed speak louder than words in an enduring relationship.

You can't talk to these people about Christ all the time, of course, lest they lock you up or divorce you. Your behavior must express much of your commitment to Christ. This behavior will be the result of your reading the Word of God and obeying it. It will be the product of the Holy Spirit's work in your life, and it will speak volumes.

Does it work? One whole family I know came to Christ because of the changed life of its junior-high-age son. The boy's behavior had so completely turned around since his conversion that his family couldn't help but see the difference. He had made contact.

Long-Term Contacts

The basic requirements for building up a long-term contact are these:

1. *Care.* Exercise great care in living consistently and attractively before the other person.

2. *Dare.* You will need more courage to witness over a long period to someone close than to speak to a stranger.

3. *Share.* If you want to make a lasting impression, share yourself with the person. Get involved in his interests, get your shoulder under his burdens, and be genuinely glad when he has a success.

▼

4. *Pray.* Don't discount the effectiveness of prayer in the preparation of people's hearts for the Good News.

Once you feel you are making some kind of consistent impression on the people close to you, one of two things will happen. Either they will come to you asking questions, or you will go to them asking questions. You will need lots of wisdom and tact, but when people begin to recognize you for what you are, they may well come to you for help.

When I was a businessman, a number of men came to me when they had spiritual needs—simply because a contact had been made which did not threaten them. When they wanted to go further, it was quite easy for them. You should aim to build this kind of long-term contact. Some, however, will never come to you. When you think the time is ripe, go to them and ask whether you might share something that is very important to you. If they respect you because of the relationship you have built with them, it is unlikely they will refuse to listen.

Don't be in too big a hurry with those you see every day. If you get after them too quickly and crudely, you may well close their ears and minds for a long time. I know wives who have come to Christ and have immediately lowered the boom on their unsuspecting, unconverted husbands. These husbands are often understandably unenthused about their wives turned evangelists; a little tact and patience go a long way!

The same is true when dealing with long-time friends. Often a person loses friends when he or she makes a commitment to Christ. Sometimes this is because the friendship is so superficial that the non-Christian cannot rejoice in the Christian's new-found happiness. Often, however, it is because the Christian loses contact with the old friend—either due to fresh involvements (more meetings than movies) or a feeling that friendship with non-Christians violates the Biblical teaching on "separation."

But we should never confuse "separation" with "isolation." Jesus showed the difference between having no part in the sinner's sin (separation) and having no part in the sinner's life

73

(isolation). He was always separated from sin, but never isolated from sinners; the Hater of Sin was the Friend of Sinners. So make sure you don't lose your friends because of your actions; but be prepared to lose some of them because they reject your Lord and your life-style.

Short-Term Contacts
Many opportunities to present Christ probably come your way daily in casual contacts. One former businessman, for instance, never served a customer without first telling him or her about Christ. "Right," you may be thinking. "That's why he's a *former* businessman." I would share those sentiments except that I know he was a *successful* businessman—who retired at age 62 to do missionary work among Muslims in North Africa. That's an unusual case, but it points out that even in everyday business life there are short-term contacts in which Christ can be shared. Remember, of course, that you're being paid to do your job, not to share the Gospel—so don't take advantage of your employer!

Traveling also presents opportunities to share Christ. Often fellow travelers will talk if you are patient and courteous. Visits to hospitals and other institutions can yield openings for witness as well.

One important thing about these casual contacts is that in God's eyes they are not casual. God says that if people really seek Him with all their hearts, they will find Him (Proverbs 8:17). But most people need someone to help them find God. If you can think of the world as being full of seekers and God as knowing every one of them and organizing circumstances so these seekers find helpers, you'll probably see where you fit into a divine plan. If you tell the Lord you are "on call" all the time, eagerly awaiting the opportunity to help seekers find Him, He will send some your way.

The Art of Conversation
If you want to get the message across to people, sooner or later you must get into conversation with them. I realize that some people are more gifted than others when it comes to talking; but

unless you have a serious impediment of some kind, you have the ability to say what you think. Settle for the fact that while you may not be an orator or an intellectual, you still know how to explain a recipe or describe what happened in a ball game.

That means you can engage in conversation that will witness to Jesus Christ. There is no basic difference in talking to people about Irish stew, American football, or the Lord, except for the subject matter. In all cases you have to know some facts, gain people's attention, assume they are interested, use words to explain, and answer questions that might arise.

True, talking to people about their eternal destiny is indescribably solemn. Those who talk about spiritual realities must be aware that they are meddling with souls. This is enough to freeze the most fluent tongues, but thankfully there is another consideration. Over and over Scripture assures us that the Lord gives His people the words to say. "I have put my words in your mouth" (Jeremiah 1:9, NIV). "I will help you speak and will teach you what to say" (Exodus 4:12, NIV). "It will not be you speaking, but the Spirit of your Father speaking through you" (Matthew 10:20, NIV).

Understanding this can deliver you from being careless on the one hand and uptight on the other. You can't be glib when you understand the solemnity of it all, but you needn't be petrified when you grasp the promise of God's help.

Here are a few skills you'll need to develop in order to have effective conversations about the Lord:

1. *Learn how to participate in ordinary conversation.* Many people think Christians are bores because they have only one topic of conversation. Often these critics have grounds for their criticism. To make sure no one can say this about you, be alert to what is going on around you; take time to formulate opinions about current events. When the conversation veers in the direction of these subjects, be ready to share your opinions. In this way you can earn the right to be heard when you want to direct the conversation toward Christ.

2. *Learn how to start conversations about spiritual issues.* Don't

assume that witnessing opportunities will always be served up to you on a plate. Often they have to be initiated. Remember how the Lord started the conversation with the woman at the well as recorded in John 4:7? He asked the woman for a drink. She was startled because it was not the "done thing" for a man to start a conversation with a woman in those days. As a result of His initiative, the whole city of Sychar was reached.

There are at least three ways to start a conversation. In the first, a general remark is made with the intention of leading into a fuller conversation. "Hello, how are you today?" spoken to someone lying in a hospital bed can elicit a recounting of ills, which in turn can lead to a discussion of the whole subject of suffering and God's role in it.

A second effective way to start a conversation is to ask the person, "What do you do?" He may answer, "Do you mean what is my job?" You can reply, "Well, that's part of it. I'm just interested in people, and I like to know what interests them." They usually tell you, then ask what *you* do. That's where it gets easy, because you can always tell them about your job, your hobbies, and your interest in the work of the Lord.

A third conversation starter is to "set somebody up." Great care should be exercised if you do this kind of thing. Sometimes when I see a person reading the paper, I say, "More bad news?"

"Yes," he or she replies. "What else is there?" I think you know the answer to *that* question.

Of course, there are more structured ways of doing this, such as going up to people and saying, "Have you heard of the Four Spiritual Laws?" If they say no, you know what to say and get into your presentation. If they growl, "Yes, I've heard them 999 times, and if anyone else mentions them to me I'll separate his head from his torso," then you must adapt!

3. *Learn how to have a discussion without getting into a fight.* This is more easily said than done if you have my kind of temperament. I love arguments, but I have given them up for the sake of the Kingdom. I could usually make my opponent look foolish even if I couldn't beat him in the argument, but I definitely didn't lead people to Christ that way.

76

4. *Learn to handle questions adequately.* Note that I didn't say, "Learn all the answers." I have a problem with people who know all the answers, because frankly, I don't think God has given us all the answers. There are also some questions that don't merit answers; no doubt you've come across the wise guy who wants you to be his straight man—not his answer man.

Try to sense the attitude of a questioner before attempting to answer his or her question. For example, "Where did Cain get his wife?" can be asked and answered in different ways. When Mr. Wise Guy asks me that old query as if he thought of it, I sometimes say, "I'm sorry, I don't know. I wasn't invited to the wedding." But if this issue is a real problem with the questioner, I would probably give a straight answer: "Shocking as it may seem, he presumably married his sister because there wasn't anybody else."

The sooner you come to terms with the fact that you do not know all the answers—and probably never will—the sooner you will feel at ease with people. If you don't know, say so. If you aren't sure, say, "I think the answer lies in this area, but quite honestly, I'm not sure." If you have a certain ambivalence, admit it. Once I had to give the answer, "Well, some say this and others say this . . . but honestly, I'm not too impressed with any of these answers, and I would be more inclined to think this."

A word of caution: I am not suggesting that you should be less than dogmatic when the Scripture is clear and plain. But neither should you feel it necessary to be dogmatic when Scripture isn't.

Helping Someone to Receive Christ

Fishermen rarely get excited about *influencing* fish. It's *landing* fish that's important to them. So it is with witnesses. They think in terms of bringing their witness to a conclusion, to bring people to commit themselves to Christ.

Not everyone is going to become a believer, of course. Not everyone to whom we witness will be ready to make a commitment. But if we keep sharing, sooner or later someone will come our way who wants to finalize something! When that happens, many witnesses turn chicken. Here are some of the reasons why:

1. *Fear.* The consequences of a Christian conversion are frightening to some people, and often the person witnessing is more aware of this than the one about to make a commitment.

2. *Doubts.* Self-doubt can be paralyzing at a time of spiritual conflict. Suddenly you're confronted with a person who wants to be led to Christ; he or she is really going to step out of darkness into light, from the power of Satan to God, from death to life. The recording angel's pen is poised, the angelic choir director's baton is raised, Heaven waits for the repentant sinner's prayer—and you can't go through with it!

You feel unworthy to be involved in something so momentous, too inexperienced not to foul it up; so you back off and say, "Well, don't rush things. Why not go away and think about it, talk to your parole officer (or wife) about it? Maybe we can have another chat sometime." Or you doubt the person's sincerity; maybe he doesn't know enough to make an intelligent decision, after all.

3. *Ignorance.* You just don't know how to bring the process to a conclusion. One approach I've found helpful is to ask three direct questions of the person to whom I've been explaining the Gospel:

- Do you need Christ?
- Do you want Christ?
- Are you willing to receive Christ?

By asking these questions, you address the person's mind, emotions, and will—and have the opportunity to further clarify what it means to become a Christian.

Suppose you are confronted by someone who has convinced you he needs Christ, wants Christ, and is willing to receive Christ. What then? You will probably need to help the person pray, just as a minister prompts a couple to repeat its vows at a wedding.

The prayer should be short and to the point. Though I have no set way of doing it, I believe a prayer of this kind should always include admission of need, a statement of repentance, an expression of trust and dependence, and a note of thanksgiving. It might sound like this: "Thank You for loving me enough to die for me, Lord Jesus. I acknowledge that I have sinned, and I ask You please to forgive me. I also know I'm not strong enough to live as I ought to, but I understand that You are prepared to come into my life by Your Spirit to give me new strength. Please do this right away. I ask You to be my Lord and my Savior. Thank You for hearing this prayer. Thank You for answering it, and thank You for all You will do in me, for me, and with me in the future. Amen."

Following Through
Right after praying to receive Christ, many people are desperately unsure of themselves. Some will feel relief; others will laugh; still others will cry. But most will look at you with a "now what?" expression on their faces.

There are many things that can be said about discipling new converts, but for purposes of this book let's condense them to the following highlights:

1. Help them to be clear about what has happened.
2. Encourage them to thank the Lord for what He has done.
3. Give them an opportunity to tell someone else what has happened.
4. Give them simple, clear Christian literature they can take away to read.
5. Arrange to have further contact.
6. Introduce them to things Christians do, such as going to church, reading the Bible, praying, and helping others—and do these things *with* them.
7. Take an interest in what interests them, including hobbies, to show that Christians are whole people—and not merely animated Bible machines!

CHAPTER 12

▼

LIVING CHRIST THROUGH THE WEEK

by Stuart

A well-dressed businessman, a new Christian, came to my office recently. He told me he wanted to serve the Lord "full-time." When I began to ask questions to see what he had in mind, I discovered he was unhappy with his current job; he thought he would enjoy being in some kind of ministry. He was understandably excited about his newfound faith, so it was a delight to listen to his testimony and share his joy. But it was harder to tell him some things that could dampen his enthusiasm.

First I had to tell him that no one should go into "full-time Christian work" just because he or she is having difficulties in the "secular world." Christian work is full of problems, too, some of them so surprising you might not believe me if I told you about them!

Second, I took great care to explain that he should not think of his work as "secular" and inferior to full-time Christian work. True, God sometimes calls people to devote all their time to ministry or missionary work. But He never suggests that their work is in some way more significant or important than the things He has called others to do.

The Value of Work
A lot of people think only clergymen are "called," and the rest of the folks just drift into what they do. We should never forget, however, that Jesus spent only three of His 33 years on earth in

"full-time service." The rest of the time He was busy learning a trade and practicing it in Nazareth. That alone gives us reason to feel that "secular" employment is *not* less significant in the eyes of God.

Of course, God the Father is not averse to work, either. In six days of hard work He created all things; on the seventh He took the day off. He also made it clear to Adam and Eve that He did not expect them to sit around all day singing hymns and writing love poems; He put them to work doing all kinds of tasks.

Things started to go wrong when man sinned. One of the results was that work became a burden. What had previously been pleasurable—*everything* had been pleasurable—became onerous. Sweat, thistles, backache, and blisters became the order of the day. But this was not because there was something wrong with work. It was because there was something wrong with human beings.

When Christ came, He worked to turn back the consequences of the Fall. Those consequences are not totally reversed yet, but there is enough blessing in Christ's redemption to make life much less difficult than it would be without Him. This includes work! In other words, believers do not have to look on work as drudgery, but as something important because God intended people to work.

Work and the Glory of God

The third point I shared with the businessman in my office was this: If he could see his work as something in which the Lord took pleasure, it would help his attitude. The man replied that he couldn't see how God was at all concerned about whether or not he sold a manufacturer a pump! The rest of the conversation went a little like this:

"Well," I said, "try thinking of it this way. All the abilities you would use to sell a pump—making contact, communicating information, motivating a sale, arranging a delivery—are God-given. When you use them, you are glorifying God."

He shook his head. "I can see how God is glorified when you use your God-given ability to preach, or when birds use their

God-given ability to sing. But I still can't see what's so great about *my* talents." As soon as the words were out of his mouth, he realized what he'd been thinking. "Oh. I must have thought that only 'special' abilities are God-given, and 'ordinary' abilities come from some other source."

When I inquired as to the whereabouts of this mythical other source, the man grinned. "OK," he said. "I guess what you mean is that all that I am came from Him—and that when I use what I am I give credit to Him!"

He was quite right. I proceeded to tell him the story of a girl who used to work making tapes of our messages. It was particularly boring work, but she had placed a sign over her workbench that said, "Quality control means finish every tape as if you were going to put it into the wounded hands of Jesus." That girl knew the value of work and how even the most "mundane" job can glorify God.

The Value of Earning Money
Fourth, I reminded this businessman that it was an honorable thing for him to provide for his family. He knew all too well that the way he provided was by working and earning money. It pleased him, though, to think about the fact that the Lord was delighted each time he brought home a check that would help put a roof over his kids' heads, a dress on his wife's back, and a bone in his dog's dish.

Fifth, we talked about the principle outlined in Ephesians 4:28 (NIV): "He who has been stealing must steal no longer, but must work, doing something useful with his own hands, *that he may have something to share with those in need*" (italics added). Here Paul shows that the products of work are to be shared with those who need them.

Thus the worker in the "secular" world has the chance to honor the Lord in his or her work, provide for the family, and help others. Imagine the joy that can infuse an "ordinary" job if the worker looks at it as a way to help some desperate soul survive in another part of the world! What job could be more meaningful?

Work and Witness

By now my friend was about ready to go back to work! But I wanted to remind him of one more point: The worker who acquits himself or herself well in the "secular" world opens the door to witness there. That worker can tell others what it is that sets him or her apart from those whose work motives are less than noble—and whose work attitudes are less than sweet.

That doesn't mean, of course, that we should spend company time preaching. There is nothing very spiritual about talking theology when your employer is paying you to bake bread! But there is something wonderfully spiritual about doing a hard day's work for a fair day's pay with a joyful attitude—and having a ready explanation during coffee break.

Christians who put the "sacred" and "secular" together in that way need never say, "Thank God it's Friday!" Instead they can have such a good time in worship and service on Sunday that they're eager to return to the marketplace on Monday to serve the Lord there. In fact, some Christians like that have been heard to shout as they leap out of bed on Monday morning, "Thank God it's Monday!"

APPENDIX

SUGGESTIONS FOR GROUP STUDY

This book, including the following 13-session discussion guide, is designed for use with the video series, *What It Means to Be a Christian,* featuring Stuart and Jill Briscoe. The video series is available from the David C. Cook Publishing Co, 850 N. Grove Ave., Elgin, IL 60120; call 1-800-323-7543 to order.

If you're leading the discussion, you'll want to see that each group member has a copy of this book. Preview the video before each session to make sure you know where to stop and start the tape as noted in the session outlines. And feel free to adapt the sessions to the needs and wants of your own group!

SESSION 1
WHY I AM A CHRISTIAN

Session Aim: To help group members understand what a Christian is, why Christ deserves their allegiance, and to evaluate their own willingness to relate to Him on His terms.

Chapter Summary
Stuart explains that a Christian is a person who has a relationship with Christ. But the relationship must be on Christ's terms, not ours. Christ demands repentance, faith, and commitment; He desires, deserves, and demands our allegiance.

God made us so we could know and enjoy Him. Our estrangement from Him grieves Him; He has provided through Christ a way to restore fellowship. The role of the other Person of the Trinity, the Holy Spirit, is to stimulate, clarify, encourage, and prick our consciences. Stuart—and we—are drawn by God's desire to have fellowship; we respond to His rescue of us; and we submit to His authority.

Video Summary
As Stuart points out, the word "Christian" is used only three times in Scripture. The word originally described someone who *belonged* to Christ. Today, however, it is culturally accepted to call yourself a Christian yet have no interest in Christ and no relationship with Him.

Stuart describes the process through which he came to personal faith in Jesus. "I cannot remember a time when I was not aware of Jesus Christ," he says, but notes that this awareness did not automatically make him a Christian. At age seven he suddenly realized that he was not a Christian and asked his mother how to become one. After her explanation of Revelation 3:20, he decided that he needed and wanted Christ and was willing to do whatever Christ wanted. Following a time of rebellion against his parents' style of Christianity, Stuart joined the Marines at age 18 and was forced to think through what Christianity is all about—which led to a maturing of his faith.

The important thing, says Stuart, is not that you know *when* you became a Christian; it's that you know you *are* one. For Stuart, Christ's victory over sin, death, and hell have shown the Lord's authority to desire, demand, and deserve our allegiance. Since Christianity is made up of sinners, we must look to Christ Himself for conclusive evidence that Christianity is true.

Session Outline

1. Get-acquainted time. Ask each person to share his or her nickname or last name and explain its meaning or origin. After learning a little about each other in this way, point out the fact that *Christian* is a name with special meaning as well.

2. Show the video. Play Stuart's 15-minute segment entitled, "Why I Am a Christian." Discuss it along the following lines:

a. Look up the Bible's three uses of the word *Christian* (Acts 11:26; 26:28; and I Peter 4:16). How do these verses imply that being a Christian requires a commitment or decision?

b. How does the way in which Stuart received Christ differ from the experiences of those in your group? How is it similar? Have a few group members or "outsiders" who believed at an early age talk about the advantages and disadvantages of "growing up Christian."

3. Discuss the chapter. Does Christ deserve our allegiance? Assign study teams or individuals to read the following passages and tell how they show that Christ is who He claims to be.

a. Fulfilled prophecies: Micah 5:2 and Matthew 2:1; Isaiah 61:1, 2 and Luke 4:16-21; Zechariah 11:12 and Matthew 26:15; Psalm 22:18 and Mark 15:24.

b. Miracles performed: Matthew 4:23, 24; John 6:9-14; 11:38-44; Mark 5:1-17.

c. His attributes: Matthew 18:20; Mark 11:2-4; Matthew 28:18.

d. The testimonies of others: Matthew 16:16; 17:5; John 1:1, 34; Acts 9:19, 20; Mark 15:39; Matthew 8:28, 29.

e. His Resurrection: Romans 1:3, 4.

4. *Apply the truth.* Are group members attracted to Christ? Have them write a "letter" to Him, telling Him either (1) what about Him makes them want to commit themselves to Him, or (2) what questions they would like answered before they could commit themselves to Him. Those who are willing can read their letters to the group. Encourage those with questions to talk with you or other group members after the session; ask everyone to read chapter 2 for next week.

SESSION 2
BECOMING A CHRISTIAN

Session Aim: To help group members identify their assumptions about what Christians are like, understand the process of receiving Christ, and consider receiving Him if they have not done so.

Chapter Summary
Jill describes how she came to receive Christ as Savior when she was 19 years old. A fellow hospital patient used Scripture references to explain to her the following four points:
  (1) All have sinned;
  (2) Sin leads to death;
  (3) Jesus died for us; and
  (4) We need to accept the gift of salvation.
Jill also points out that through Christ we can have assurance of the following:
  (1) Forgiveness;
  (2) Eternal life; and
  (3) Provision for our earthly needs.

Video Summary
Jill came from an unchurched family. Her early view of Christians could be represented by this acrostic:
  Churchgoers
  Hypocrites
  Rule makers
  Insecure
  Spoilsports
  Troubled
  Idiots
  Annoying
  Naive

But Janet, the girl who witnessed to Jill in the hospital, didn't fit that cynical formula. From this girl Jill learned that "I was a sinner; Heaven was shut to me; Christ had died to open that door; and if I wanted to, I could walk through that door."

After she received Christ, Jill had a new view of what a Christian is like:

Christ's one
Happy
Right
Indwelt (by the Spirit)
Secure
Triumphant
Intelligent
Authority (having a sense of who you are and who God is)
Neat (having friends who love you because you love Jesus)

Session Outline

1. Do an acrostic. Post large sheets of paper on the wall or have smaller ones available on a table. As group members enter, ask them to write an acrostic on the word *Christian* that shows either how they see Christians or how they think non-Christians see them.

2. Show the video. Play just the first five or so minutes of Jill's segment entitled, "Becoming a Christian"—stopping the tape after she says, "As I was running around Cambridge . . . I felt I knew better than everybody else." Discuss Jill's preconversion acrostic. Do any in your group identify with her assumptions? Why might non-Christians feel that way? Are there reasons for the view of Christians as hypocrites, spoilsports, etc.?

Then play the next three minutes of the tape, stopping it after Jill says, "That's when I began to learn that *Christian* was not all those negative things that I thought *Christian* was." Discuss the process of becoming a Christian. What drew Jill to want to become a Christian? Can any group members describe how to become a Christian without using such "religious" terms as *salvation, born again, confess, accept,* or *receive?* Have them try. Then break into small groups to consider the following questions and the verses that answer them.

a. Was Christ's death voluntary? (John 10:17, 18)
b. For whom did Christ die? (Romans 5:8)
c. What did Christ's death accomplish? (Hebrews 9:26-28)
d. What are the results of sin? (Romans 6:23)
e. How can a person have eternal life? (John 3:16)

Finally, show the rest of the "Becoming a Christian" video. Discuss Jill's revised acrostic on the word *Christian*. Do your group members agree that these qualities are typical of Christians? Which traits are automatic at conversion, and with which do we often continue to struggle? If God takes time to grow Christians (as He does oaks from acorns), where do your students see themselves in the process? Are they acorns, saplings, oaks—or something else entirely?

3. Make it personal. Have each person read John 3:16 to a partner. The person to whom it is read should then explain to the partner how things would be different for him or her if God had not sent His Son. Close with prayer and an offer to talk further with anyone who would like to know more about how to become a Christian. Encourage group members to read chapter 3 for next week.

SESSION 3
STUDYING THE BIBLE: WHY BOTHER?

Session Aim: To help group members understand the importance of personal Bible study, and to identify and overcome impediments to study.

Chapter Summary
Stuart points out that in order to benefit from Bible study, you have to be motivated. Many people aren't motivated to get into the Bible because they don't realize how unique a Book it is. Four unique qualities of Scripture are listed:
1. The Bible is inspired by the Holy Spirit.
2. The Bible is the only way of knowing how to be reconciled with God.
3. The Bible is the only place to find out how to continue in the Christian life.
4. The Bible is the only place to discover what will happen in the future.

Stuart also mentions that two ingredients are necessary for effective Bible study: (1) the correct attitude toward Scripture, and (2) help from the Holy Spirit.

Video Summary
Since Stuart has always been a voracious reader, Bible reading has not been too difficult a habit for him to pick up. He realizes, however, that it's harder for those who don't enjoy reading. Still, *all* Christians need to get into the Bible in order to grow spiritually.

Three reasons to study the Bible are presented:
1. In the Bible, God has taken the trouble to speak; we should take the trouble to listen.
2. The Bible is useful for instruction and reproof—letting us know what we should and should not do.
3. The end product of Bible study is spiritual maturity; if we're not interested in that, we need to check our relationship with God.

Session Outline

1. *The Bible: a unique Book.* Bring three or four books of different kinds (the Yellow Pages, a textbook, a Christian self-help book, etc.) and show them to the group. Ask: What types of questions can be answered by these books? How are they limited? How are they different from God's Word?

Ask group members to describe the most important or meaningful letters they ever got in the mail. Were they important because of the sender, the content, or both? Why is the Bible—a letter from God—so important?

2. *Show the video.* Play only the first five or so minutes of Stuart's "Studying the Bible" in this session. Stop the tape as soon as he says, "Obviously, there's much more we could say on the subject of generating desire for the Bible, but that's all we have time for right now." How many of your group members would call themselves avid readers like Stuart? How many don't read much at all? How do our overall reading habits affect our view of Bible study?

Brainstorm other reasons why it's usually hard to start studying the Bible. Is the Bible "user-friendly"? Why or why not? Have the more experienced members of the group found ways to make Bible study less formidable? Ask them to share their discoveries.

3. *Talk about the chapter.* Discuss the Bible's four unique qualities as listed by Stuart. Why are they important? Without the Bible, where might we turn for the information it contains? Do Christians always go to the Bible for this information? Why or why not?

4. *The Bible speaks for itself.* Answer the following questions as a group by studying the verses listed.

a. How does God's Word describe itself? What do these descriptions say about the role of the Bible in our lives? (Luke 8:11; Psalm 119:105; Jeremiah 23:29; Ephesians 6:17; Psalm 19:8-10; I Peter 2:2)

b. What should we do with the Word of God? (Isaiah 34:16; II Timothy 2:15; Psalm 1:1, 2; Acts 17:11; Psalm 119:11; James 1:22)

c. In what way is the Bible valuable to us? (II Timothy 3:15, 16; Psalm 119:130; Romans 15:4)

5. *Self-examination.* Point out Stuart's assertion that we need to check our relationship with God if we're not interested in growing spiritually through Bible study. Break into informal conversation groups to discuss this statement, and to pray for each other's desire to study God's Word. Have students read chapter 4 for next week.

SESSION 4
STUDYING THE BIBLE: TOOLS FOR DIGGING

Session Aim: To acquaint group members with basic tools for Bible study, and to provide experience in using them.

Chapter Summary
What helps do you need to study the Bible? Stuart recommends the following:

1. A Bible—a readable version with readable type and room for notes in the margin.

2. A notebook—to preserve your discoveries, encourage consistency in your study, and track your growth.

3. A concordance—an index to help you find verses and words.

4. Colored pencils—for underlining verses according to theme, which is a memory aid and organizing device.

5. A Bible dictionary—gives a fuller understanding of passages you study.

6. A commentary—for help when you get stuck, not as a substitute for studying the Bible itself.

Video Summary
In addition to covering much of the material found in the chapter, Stuart describes study Bibles, which combine a number of helps—such as maps and notes—with the text. He also urges studying the Bible on a daily basis.

Session Outline
1. *Breaking the code.* Make a list of not-too-familiar Biblical terms on the board or a flip chart. These may get you started: *ephod, lintel, Jubilee, Joses, propitiation, mercy seat.* See how many of them can be explained by group members. Note that we often need help in deciphering Biblical words, phrases, and passages.

97

Explain that later in the session you'll use special tools to do just that.

2. *Show the video.* Start the "Studying the Bible" tape where you left off last week. Play only the next six minutes, stopping it again after Stuart says, "You can go on and get Bible dictionaries . . . but we probably don't need to concern ourselves about that right now." That's all you'll play this week. Ask: How does the way we study the Bible affect our understanding of it? How can our interpretation of Bible words and passages affect our beliefs and actions?

3. *Summarize the chapter.* To review and complement the video, have one or more group members name the items Stuart recommends as useful in Bible study. Take a straw poll to find out how many students have these tools at home (or with them). Do they use them? How?

4. *Trying out tools.* Split into four groups. Give each group one of the following: concordance, Bible dictionary, commentary, or study Bible. Have each group list six features of the study tool it's been given, and three ways in which it could be used to aid Bible understanding. Then each group should use its study aid to find out all it can about the terms listed on the board at the beginning of the session. Results should be shared with the large group. If time allows, have the groups switch study helps and find out all they can about the Last Supper (or other Biblical event or topic) in five minutes.

5. *Underlining without pencils.* To show how thematic underlining of verses in different colors works, read Titus 3 aloud (with students following in their Bibles). Pause after each verse to allow group members to call out the theme(s) contained therein (see Stuart's system as described in the chapter).

6. *Testimonial.* Have an older member of your congregation (whom you've contacted beforehand) tell the group how he or

98

she has been helped by daily Bible study and keeping a notebook. Find two or more volunteers (probably beforehand) who will agree to study Philippians 1 (or another brief chapter) daily this week and keep a notebook—and who will report the results to the group next week. Urge everyone to read chapter 5 for next time.

SESSION 5
STUDYING THE BIBLE: THREE WAYS

Session Aim: To encourage group members to study the Bible for themselves—by giving them hands-on experience in three popular study methods.

Chapter Summary
The first type of Bible study Stuart describes is a *book study.* The student chooses a book of the Bible and reads it, preferably in more than one version. Then he or she looks for natural divisions in the text, according to subject, and divides the book accordingly. Finally he or she uses this outline as a skeleton upon which to fill in more detailed insights.

A second approach is the *word study.* The student uses a concordance or Bible dictionary to find the meaning of a word. A concordance will also list other verses in which the word occurs; studying these verses can unlock additional meaning.

A third type of study is the *character study.* This approach is especially helpful in showing what God can do with ordinary people. The student chooses a Biblical character who interests him or her (but not one about whom there is an overwhelming amount of material, at least in the beginning). Then the student seeks to answer from Scripture the following questions about that character:
1. Who was he (she)?
2. What did he do, say, think, desire?
3. Where did he do what he did?
4. Why was he the person he was?
5. Whom did he affect by his life?

Video Summary
Stuart concentrates mainly on the book study, recommending that the beginner start with a short book like Philippians. The student should read the book once, twice, and three times to get the sense of it—and then determine the theme of the book.

Next the student may give a title of his or her own to the book, based on its theme. Finally the book should be divided into sections along its natural division lines, and those sections titled.

Session Outline

1. *Volunteers' report.* If some of your group studied the Bible daily and kept a notebook this week, ask them to share how they did it and what they learned. Encourage them to keep at it, and urge others to join them.

2. *Object lesson.* Have three group members choose an object in the room—without telling anyone else what it is. One should describe the object to the group strictly in terms of how much it weighs; another according to the object's texture; and the third in terms of the sound the object would make if it fell to the floor. The rest of the group tries to guess the object after each description. When the object has been guessed or revealed, explain that just as we need more than one kind of description to picture a physical object, more than one Bible study method helps us get a clearer understanding of Scripture.

3. *Show the video.* Pick up Stuart's "Studying the Bible" tape where you left off last time. Play it to the end. How do the methods Stuart describes differ from those your students have used alone and in home Bible studies? What advantages are there to systematic study over the "Well, how does this verse strike you?" method?

4. *Retrace the steps.* Have group members, using the chapter, outline on the board or a flip chart the steps to all three Bible study methods. Make sure the outline is legible and visible to the whole group for the next activity.

5. *Triple-threat Bible study.* Split into three groups, one for each Bible study method. The book-study group should study the Epistle to Philemon; have the word-study group look at the

word *grace*; and assign the character-study group to examine the apostle Paul (using only the Book of Philemon). Introduce the study by explaining that Onesimus was a runaway slave who had become a Christian, and Philemon was his Christian master. Make last week's study helps available, too. After allowing plenty of time for the study, have the groups share results and see how the three types of study provide a more complete view of Scripture.

6. *Signing the commitment papers.* Give group members the opportunity to consider signing "commitment papers" (certificate-style sheets you've prepared) which affirm that they will study a specific Biblical book, word, or character by a definite date—either on their own or with other group members. Give students a week to consider this step; let those who are willing to sign say so at the next session. In the meantime, everyone should read chapter 6.

SESSION 6
LEARNING TO PRAY:
AN INTRODUCTION

Session Aim: To help group members grasp the nature and purpose of prayer, and its vital role in their relationship to God.

Chapter Summary
Stuart explains that prayer is the talking part of one's relationship with God. The Lord speaks to us through the Bible; we respond in prayer. We should pray for the following reasons:
(1) To develop our relationship with God,
(2) Because Christ has told us to, and
(3) To follow the example of Christ.
When should we pray? Regularly, spontaneously, and continually.

Video Summary
Prayer, says Jill, is communication. It is the speaking part of our relationship with the Lord. Prayer begins with an introduction, as do most conversations, when a person prays to receive Christ. After the introduction comes a period of discovery, in which we begin to get to know God. We can ask Him questions like these: Who are You? Where do You live? What do You believe? In return, He will answer—through His written Word.

Session Outline
1. *Mapping our prayer lives.* Post or draw on the board a map of your town, or make a list of locations (church, kitchen, school, bedroom, car, restaurant, etc.). Have group members rate on a scale of one to ten the ease they feel in praying in those spots. Why do they feel more at ease than in others? Is the style, length, or substance of their prayers likely to change from place to place? How? Would they describe themselves as satisfied, struggling, or shamed over their prayer practices?

103

2. *Show the video.* Play the first seven or so minutes of Jill's segment, "Learning to Pray." Stop the tape after she says, "It was as He disclosed that to me in the Scriptures that I began to talk back to Him about those things." (The rest of this segment will be used in the next session.) Discuss the video along the following lines:

a. What is Jill's definition of prayer? Come up with your own symbol for prayer (other than a microphone, which Jill uses).

b. How is prayer like and unlike a human conversation? How is it easier? More difficult?

c. When you were introduced to God by praying to receive Christ, what was your prayer like? Has your praying changed since then? How?

3. *Mock debate.* Take the role of a person who thinks prayer is pointless. Challenge group members to make a case for praying, using Stuart's chapter, the Bible, and any other resources they can muster.

4. *Study teams.* Divide the group in half. Have one half answer the question, "What are the conditions of prayer?" by studying the following passages and reporting their findings to the whole group: John 14:13; I John 5:14, 15; Romans 8:16, 26; James 1:5,7; Colossians 4:2. Have the other half do the same with the question, "What are some hindrances to prayer?" and these verses: I John 3:22; I Peter 3:6, 7; Matthew 5:23, 24; James 4:2, 3; Psalm 66:18.

Discuss the teams' findings. How do God's conditions for effective prayer help us to mature spiritually? What do these conditions tell us about the kind of relationship God wants to have with us? What additional hindrances to prayer have your group members discovered through experience, and what did they do about them?

5. *Discovering God through prayer.* What would your students like to ask God? Encourage them to find the answers through the two-way "conversation" of prayer and Bible study. Have

each group member write down two or three questions for God and put them in the back of his or her Bible as a reminder to pray and study to discover answers this week. Remind students to read chapter 7 for next time.

SESSION 7
LEARNING TO PRAY:
GETTING TO KNOW GOD

Session Aim: To encourage group members to grow in their relationship to God by praying Biblically and effectively.

Chapter Summary

Stuart uses the following acrostic to describe Biblical prayer:
    Praise
    Repentance
    Asking
    Yourself

Thus Biblical, effective prayer begins with praising God—praising Him for Himself, for blessings He has given us, for His answers to our prayers. It continues with repentance, which restores fellowship with the Lord which has been broken by sin.

Then it is appropriate to ask things of God—a step we often put first and foremost. Looking at the Lord's Prayer as a model, Stuart recommends praying as follows:

1. That God's name be honored.
2. That God's Kingdom be completed.
3. That God's will be implemented.
4. For physical needs (such as daily bread).
5. For social needs (such as forgiving others and being forgiven).
6. For spiritual needs (such as deliverance from temptation).

Finally comes prayer for yourself. It is fine to pray for yourself, but it should also be with God's glory in mind. To reverse his recommended order, says Stuart, would not be praying; it would be yarping!

Video Summary

Prayer, says Jill, is *debate* as well as introduction and discovery.

It is a two-way conversation in which we get to know God. Prayer has been called the debating chamber of the soul; it served that function for Jesus and the Father in the Garden of Gethsemane.

Sometimes it seems hard to fit prayer into our schedules, but when we're in love we find time to be together and get to know each other. As a busy young mother, for example, Jill found that she could have her "quiet times" of prayer and Bible reading— by climbing into the playpen and putting her children outside of it!

Jill encourages believers to work on three requirements of communication—honesty, listening, and coming to a consensus of opinion (understanding)—as they pray. She also states that prayer should be a *delight*. Sometimes the Christian who is getting to know God doesn't even need words to pray in order to share deep sorrows and joys.

Session Outline

1. Show the video. Pick up where you left off last week with Jill's "Learning to Pray" segment. Play the rest of the tape. Discuss the problems of finding a place and time to pray. Do students see themselves in the Introduction, Discovery, or Debate stage of prayer—or in more than one stage at once? Why? Is prayer a *delight* for your group members? If not, what would have to change to make it so?

2. Praying or yarping? Call on one or more group members to summarize Stuart's chapter, especially the meaning of his acrostic on the word *pray*. Pass out sheets of paper on which students should list 10 or 12 things they've talked to God about in the past month or two. Then have them write a *P, R, A,* or *Y* next to each item to show whether it was praise, repentance, asking for something on someone else's behalf, or asking something for yourself. What kinds of prayers predominate? Have your students been praying or "yarping"? In what areas do they need to change?

3. *A model prayer.* Read the Lord's Prayer (Matthew 6:9-13) aloud. If you haven't done so already, summarize Stuart's outline for prayer based on the Lord's Prayer. Then study the verses which come *before* this famous prayer (6:5-8). What do they say about how we should pray? What are some contemporary examples of praying to be "seen of men" and using "vain repetitions"? What are some ways to pray "in a closet" today? Why might God want us to ask Him for things even though He knows what we want?

4. *Getting to know you.* Have group members break into pairs. The goal is for each person to find out as much as possible about the other. But for one minute at a time, special conditions will be placed on the dialogue:

a. For the first minute, one partner will not have to be honest.

b. For the second minute, one partner will not have to listen.

c. For the third minute, one partner must disagree with everything the other says.

After the three minutes are up, discuss how the conditions of the conversation made it harder to get to know each other. Point out the necessity of honesty, listening, and coming to agreement in the process of getting to know God through prayer. What factors tend to keep us from being honest with God, from listening to Him, and from understanding and agreeing with Him?

5. *Prayer partners.* Keeping group members in pairs, have them spend the remaining minutes of the session listing (1) reasons to praise God and (2) prayer requests—and then telling God about these. Ask students to read chapter 8 for next week.

SESSION 8
SHOWING LOVE FOR THE CHURCH

Session Aim: To help group members understand what the Church is meant to be, and to encourage them to reflect Christ's love for the Church by committing themselves to it.

Chapter Summary
The Church, Stuart contends, is not a building. It's people— people who have a special relationship with Jesus Christ. They express their gratitude to God through such unique activities as these:

1. *Fellowship*. Christians should be characterized by sharing.

2. *Worship*. There are many styles of Christian worship, but one Lord.

3. *Stewardship*. This is an attitude which motivates Christians to use their resources, financial and otherwise, in light of the fact that those resources really belong to God.

4. *Discipleship*. The essence of discipleship is ordinary people in ordinary walks of life refusing to be pressed into the mold of society around them. They live according to the teachings and promises of Christ. Learning to be a disciple takes place best in a community—the Church.

Is the Church perfect? Not at all, says Stuart. It's made up entirely of sinners. That's why the person who looks for an ideal church is bound to be disappointed.

Video Summary
Stuart admits that he was not always enthusiastic about the Church—even when he was enthusiastic about Jesus and serving Him. But one day a friend asked him, "How could you be all in favor of Jesus Christ, and not be all in favor of what He's all in favor of?" The friend was referring to the Church, which Christ loves.

That question led Stuart to study what the Church is supposed to be. He discovered that the word from which we get "church" means "belonging to the Lord." The Church belongs to Christ, even if it's a mess. And it's not somewhere you go, it's something you are.

When mankind sinned in the Garden of Eden, Stuart says, people-to-people relationships were marred—as were relationships between God and people. God wanted to restore those human relationships, that community, so He created a brand-new one: the Church.

People in the Church have in common their relationship to Jesus and their love for one another. That love is not something sentimental, but a hard-nosed commitment. The Church should also be marked by its caring, its commitment, its cheerfulness, and its convictions. These characteristics attract others as well as honoring God.

Session Outline

1. Complete the sentence. Have each group member complete one or more of the following sentences:

a. The thing I like (or dislike) most about the Church is. . . .

b. I once changed churches because. . . .

c. My definition of *church* is. . . .

Briefly discuss the group's answers. Do they wish they could be more enthused about the Church? Are they unclear on what the Church is supposed to be? Today's session may help.

2. Show the video. Play the entire "Showing Love for the Church" segment with Stuart. Discuss it, using questions like these:

a. To whom does the Church belong?

b. Can you truly love Christ and not love His Church?

c. Why isn't the Church perfect?

d. Why doesn't God force the Church to be perfect?

3. The Church in Scripture. Assign group members to read the following verses aloud: Matthew 16:18; Colossians 1:18; Ephesians 6:23-30; Hebrews 10:24, 25. What do these verses tell us about (a) the founder of the Church, (b) the strength of the

Church, (c) the Head of the Church, (d) the future of the Church, and (e) the necessity of the Church?

Read John 13:34, 35. How should this commandment affect our view of the Church? Of other individual Christians? Can we let "all men" know that we are Christ's disciples *without* loving each other? Why or why not? What has been the reaction of non-Christians to relationships in your church? What does this say about your church?

Read Philippians 2:1-11, 14. According to Paul, how can we show love for the Church?

4. *United we stand.* On the board or a flip chart, start two columns—one headed, "By Myself," the other headed, "Together." Brainstorm areas of the Christian life which are best handled alone, those which are best dealt with in a community, and those which can be handled in either setting. Add Stuart's list of four areas from the chapter and summarize his comments.

5. *The four C's.* Discuss ways in which your church (and group) can show its caring, commitment, cheerfulness, and convictions. Be specific. How can showing these qualities start with one person? Encourage group members to follow through on concrete suggestions. Close with sentence prayers in which students thank the Lord for an aspect of His Church. Remind them to read chapter 9 for next time.

LEARNING OBEDIENCE

Session Aim: That group members, seeing how obeying God is a result of loving Him, and that obedience is part of the most satisfying kind of life, will be motivated to obey Him.

Chapter Summary
Jill explains that love and obedience are related—"married," in a way. Their "offspring" are joy, peace, and power. As we start the Christian life, we may obey simply because we're *supposed* to, but as we mature we obey for the joy of it. Jesus is the grand example of obedience to the Father.

Obedience also brings peace. Disobedience, conversely, brings guilt and turmoil. God gives us the power to obey Him *as we obey*, not before. Obeying God leads to happiness.

Video Summary
Obedience, Jill says, is doing what you're told. The trouble is that there's something in each of us that wants to rebel. It's the sin principle, and it causes us to be "off center." As Jesus indicates in John 14:15, our love for God can be measured by our obedience. In fact, obedience is a way to show love for God.

We find out what to obey by reading the Bible. The Ten Commandments are a good measuring stick for checking our obedience, as are the "greatest commandments" in Matthew 22:35-40 (love God first, your neighbor second, yourself last).

Jill says that anyone *can* be obedient; it's a question of whether we're *going* to do it. We have to decide. Jill describes a point at which she decided that whatever she felt God desired her to do she would do, whether she wanted to do it or not.

Putting God first means letting Him be Lord, giving Jesus the helm. We must also feed on the Word in order to learn obedience. Putting others second means loving people we may not like. Putting ourselves last does not mean putting ourselves down; it means loving ourselves as well, because part of being obedient is accepting ourselves as God has made us.

Session Outline

1. *Rebels without a pause.* Have group members share early childhood memories of how they once disobeyed parents. Then ask them to relate more recent incidents of disobeying Biblical principles. Do they see a pattern of rebellion against authority? How do the rebellions of a child and an adult differ? How are they alike?

2. *Show the video.* Play the first five minutes of Jill's "Learning Obedience" segment, stopping the tape after she says, "Being obedient is how we show God—or how we show Jesus—that we really love Him." Discuss: Are there other ways to show love for God? Can we show love for Him and still be disobedient? How do we try to "get around" John 14:15?

Show the next minute of the video, stopping the tape after Jill says, "The two greatest commandments are these: Love God first; love your neighbor second and love yourself last." Read the Ten Commandments (Exodus 20:1-17) and Jesus' "greatest commandments" (Matthew 22:35-40). How are the ten embodied in Jesus' statement? What are some practical ways to keep these commandments in our minds and hearts?

Finally, show the rest of the "Learning Obedience" segment. Is the decision to obey God a one-time choice? A series of choices? Does obeying become easier the more you obey? Why? What resources has God given us to help us obey?

3. *Commercials for obedience.* Split the group into thirds; each third should study one of the "children" of love and obedience—joy, peace, or power. Group members should use Jill's chapter as their reference. After several minutes of study, each team should write a TV or radio commercial "selling" obedience, using joy, peace, or power as the "consumer benefit." Regather and have the teams perform their ads.

4. *Getting ready to obey.* Close in silent prayer. Encourage students as they pray to think of specific temptations they face, and to rely on God for the power to obey Him. Read the

following verses aloud before bringing the prayer time to an end: James 4:7, 8; I Corinthians 10:13; and Philippians 4:13. Urge group members to read chapter 10 for next week.

SESSION 10
TALKING ABOUT FAITH: WHO NEEDS IT?

Session Aim: That group members will understand what a "witness" is, and why God wants them to share their faith with others.

Chapter Summary
Stuart provides the following definition of a witness: Someone who gives, by explanation and demonstration, audible and visible evidence of what he or she has seen and heard—without being deterred by the consequences. A *Christian* witness is one who, in a variety of ways, communicates the truth as it is to be found in Christ.

Why should we witness? Stuart cites these reasons:
(1) Because Christ said we would be witnesses;
(2) Because Christ Himself was a witness;
(3) Because God planned that we should be witnesses; and
(4) Because the world needs us to be witnesses.

Through our witness, Stuart points out, God can do the following:
(1) Convert a person from the error of his or her ways;
(2) Save a person's soul from death; and
(3) Hide a multitude of sins.

Stuart also cites three reasons for our frequent lack of concern over sharing our faith:
(1) Spiritual reasons (we need the Holy Spirit to open our eyes);
(2) Theological reasons (we are vague about the reality of hell); and
(3) Practical reasons (we're afraid of others' reaction, or lack how-to knowledge).

Video Summary

Jill retells the story of the demon-possessed, tomb-wandering man in Mark 5. Jesus healed the man, then told him, "Go home to your family and tell them how much the Lord has done for you, and how he has had mercy on you" (v. 19, NIV). The man did as he was instructed. We should do likewise and tell others what the Lord has done for us. When we become Christians, Jesus doesn't say, "Now that you're a Christian, come and live in Heaven with Me." He wants us to stay here and share the Good News with others.

When Jill received Christ, she made the mistake of not showing her family how the Lord had changed her. She just started preaching at them. She admits now that she should have "lived the difference" and thereby earned the right to tell why she'd changed. That isn't to say, however, that a nonverbal witness is enough; verbal explanation is needed as well.

Session Outline

1. *I've got a reason.* Have several group members name a few reasons why they're glad to be Christians. After you've heard a dozen or so reasons, observe that your students have just done something that strikes fear into the hearts of many believers—they've been *witnesses*.

2. *Defining terms.* Ask a student to read aloud from the chapter Stuart's definitions of a witness and a Christian witness. Any dissenters? Discuss: What are we communicating about the Lord by the things we do and say?

3. *Show the video.* Play the first six minutes of Jill's "Talking About Faith" segment, stopping the tape after she says, "It does say that all the people (v. 20) were amazed; it does not say that all the people were converted." Discuss: If you had been the man Jesus healed, what might you have told others? How might you have told them? What could Jill have done to be a better witness to her family?

116

4. *Why witness?* Using Stuart's chapter, summarize and discuss his reasons for witnessing. Which do your group members find most compelling? Why? Brainstorm the needs a non-Christian might have, writing them on the board or a flip chart. Which of these needs can be met in Christ?

5. *Who cares?* Summarize and discuss the reasons Stuart lists for lacking concern about witnessing. With which can your group identify? Together or in small groups, examine the following verses concerning Jesus' view of the reality of hell: Matthew 5:22; 10:28; 11:23; 13:40-42; 25:29-46; Luke 16:19-31. How is this place described? For whom is it intended? Read II Peter 3:7-9. Does God want to send people to hell? How does He want them to avoid that destination?

6. *Who, me?* Give your students this question to think about during the week: Which are more important—our reasons for not talking about faith, or the needs of non-Christians around us? Ask everyone to read chapter 11 for next time.

SESSION 11
TALKING ABOUT FAITH:
YOU CAN DO IT!

Session Aim: That group members will understand how to share their faith with others, and gain practice in doing so.

Chapter Summary

Stuart lists four kinds of workers to which believers are compared in the Bible: fishermen, ambassadors, reapers, and watchmen. Like those workers, we must make contact with those we seek to reach, "harvest," or observe; we cannot expect them to come to us. When we have long-term contacts to whom we wish to witness, it is important to care (live carefully, consistently), dare (be courageous), share (give of yourself to the other person), and pray. We should be especially tactful and patient with long-term contacts. And while being separated from the sinfulness of the world system, we should not become isolated from its people.

To share effectively with short-term contacts, we should do the following:

1. Learn the art of conversation.
2. Participate in "ordinary" conversations.
3. Start conversations about spiritual issues.
4. Discuss, but don't get into a fight.
5. Learn how to handle questions adequately.
6. Trust God to give you the words to say.

When possible, urge the person with whom you're sharing to make a commitment to Christ. To discover whether he or she is ready, ask: (1) Do you need Christ? (2) Do you want Christ? (3) Are you willing to receive Christ? If the person prays to receive Christ, follow through by helping the person to grow spiritually.

Video Summary

According to Jill, we are responsible to share our faith; we are not responsible for others' reactions. Some will accept the Gospel, and others will reject it. God can take even our witnessing *mistakes* and use them, because failure is never final for the Christian.

Jill recounts the story of the lepers who found the booty of a retreating army and realized their need to share it (II Kings 7). We, too, should not "hold our peace" concerning the "good tidings" about Jesus. We should tell people that they don't have to go to hell, they don't have to be lost.

We are ambassadors. It's a privilege, not a punishment. But we will witness only if we really *believe* what we say we believe.

Session Outline

1. Show the video. Pick up where you left off last week with the "Talking About Faith" segment. Play the rest of the segment. Then note Jill's observation that if we knew the cure for cancer, we'd tell everyone about it. What *would* your group members do if they had a cure for cancer? How would they tell others? Whom would they tell first? What if few people believed in the existence of cancer, or cancer had no symptoms? How would they spread the cure then? What can we learn from this analogy about sharing our faith?

2. Discuss the chapter. Stuart recommends ways to deal with long-term and short-term witnessing contacts. Have each group member make a list of his or her long-term contacts, plus short-term contacts he or she has had in the past month. Ask volunteers to share their lists. How could Stuart's advice be applied in these situations?

3. Back to the Book. As a group, read and study Acts 2:37-47. According to this passage, in what ways were people drawn to become Christians? How are people drawn to Christ today? Read Colossians 4:5, 6 and Matthew 5:14-17. Ask the group for examples of how we can obey these verses at home, at work, or at school.

4. *A Not-Just-Success Story.* Have a member of the group or congregation (whom you've invited beforehand) tell the group how he or she led someone to Christ—and about a time when his or her witness was a seeming failure. What has the person learned from these experiences? Would he or she agree with Jill, who says that God can use our mistakes? Why?

5. *Roleplaying.* Divide the group into twos or threes. Have group members take turns telling each other how they came to personal faith in Christ (if indeed they have). Students can ask questions of each other for clarification, but not to challenge or put down. After students have told their stories, have them pray for each other—that God will give them opportunities to talk about their faith. As students leave, give each a reminder for the week—a slip of paper on which you've copied the Great Commission (Matthew 28:19, 20). They should read chapter 12 for next time, too.

SESSION 12
LIVING CHRIST THROUGH THE WEEK

Session Aim: That your group members will see what it means to be a Christian in everyday "secular" life, particularly the workplace, and that they will want to make the most of opportunities to worship and witness in that world.

Chapter Summary
Stuart presents five reasons why working in the "secular" world is good:

1. Work has value because God intended people to work.
2. When you use the abilities God gave you, you glorify Him.
3. Providing for your family is honorable—indeed, it is commanded in Scripture.
4. Work makes wealth to share with others in need.
5. Work can provide an open door to witness.

Video Summary
Some people, Stuart says, would like to live in church all the time—where it's "warm and safe." But God doesn't want it that way. He wants us to be "in the world but not of it." It's one thing to be separated from the world's evil, but another to be isolated and insulated from its people. God wants Christians to move around in the "secular" world.

When he was a banker, Stuart wanted to do a good job but be distinctive—to show people he "marched to a different drummer." His advice for Christians who do "secular" work:

1. Be credible and natural in your witness, not obnoxious— and remember that your employer is paying you to work, not to evangelize.
2. Remember that work itself has value; in the beginning, God worked!
3. "Whatsoever ye do, do it heartily, as to the Lord, and not unto men" (Colossians 3:23). We need a high view of work; you are banking (or whatever) before the King of Kings.

4. Demonstrate a Christian ethic; "normal business proce-dure" sometimes conflicts with Biblical principles.

5. "Them that honour me I will honour," says the Lord (I Samuel 2:30). Work according to Biblical principles and God will honor your work.

6. Instead of trying to flee to "full-time Christian work," try to stay where you are—in the "secular" world.

7. Remember that "to work is to worship; to worship is to work."

Session Outline

1. *"Foreign" objects.* During the week, collect from several group members objects that represent their jobs or hobbies. Before the meeting, set the objects on a table; as students enter, see how many can guess which objects belong to which people. Point out that we often don't know much about each other's weekdays; we tend to separate our "Sunday" lives from our "secular" lives.

2. *Show the video.* Play Stuart's entire "Living Christ Through the Week" segment. Ask: How could you "march to a different drummer" as a lawyer? Service station attendant? Homemaker? Senator? Public school teacher? Mail carrier? Used car salesper-son? What experiences have group members had in this area?

3. *Workers in the Bible.* Through group study, discover the occupations of Bible characters in these verses: Acts 16:14; 18:1-3; Genesis 9:20; 13:5; 42:6; Proverbs 31:10-31; Mark 6:3, 4; Matthew 4:18; 9:9. Did these people have "secular" or "sacred" jobs? Which jobs were "ordinary," and which were "special"? Did God seem to prefer certain occupations over others? How did God use these people? What abilities did He give them? Was their "earthly" work a waste of time? Why or why not?

4. *Case study.* Ask a group member (as arranged beforehand) to tell of an ethical dilemma he or she faced at work. Let the group analyze the dilemma and offer solutions. Would the

122

proposed solutions tend to bring others to Christ or drive them away? Then allow the person who faced the problem to tell what he or she did (and perhaps *should* have done, based on Biblical principles).

5. *Days of our lives.* Pass out blank calendars for the coming month. Have group members mill around, getting each other person to autograph at least one day, until each day contains at least one signature. Ask students to pray for those who autographed their calendars on the days their signatures appear. In preparation for that, spend the last several minutes collecting prayer requests related to through-the-week concerns.

SESSION 13
REVIEW

Session Aim: That your group members will identify more specifically ways in which they can apply selected principles from this series.

Session Outline

Rather than covering a chapter or video segment, this session reviews the whole course. Instead of trying to review all 12 sessions, however, take a poll before this meeting to determine which subjects your group would like to discuss further. Which do they feel "shakiest" about? Which do they need help in applying to "real life"? Choose the top two or three topics and use the following suggestions to build your own review session.

Why I Am a Christian / Becoming a Christian

1. Salvation sermon. Study Acts 3:12-26 (Peter preaches the Gospel). Summarize Peter's message. What does he want people to do? Paraphrase in your own words.

2. Tract trek. In small groups, examine half a dozen good evangelistic tracts. How do they outline the plan of salvation? What do they promote as the benefits of being a Christian? Share results in the whole group.

Studying the Bible

1. Guided study. Using Stuart's guidelines for a book study, examine James 1 as a group. Assign those who understand the use of outlining, concordances, Bible dictionaries, underlining, etc., to lead the use of these tools, making sure they explain what they are doing. Encourage questions about the study method itself as well as the passage. Have students write their findings.

Learning to Pray

1. Praying for others. After reviewing the P.R.A.Y. acrostic, read the following passages to discover instances in which believers prayed for others—or were told to. What were the circumstances? (Genesis 20:17; Numbers 11:1, 2; I Samuel 8:6; II Kings 4:33; 19:15; Job 42:10; I Timothy 2:1, 2; II Timothy 1:3; Acts 7:59; and Ephesians 6:18-20) For whom should we pray?

2. *Newspaper prayer.* In small groups, "pray through" items from the front page section of a recent newspaper. Include praise, repentance, asking, and prayer for yourself.

Showing Love for the Church
1. *Treating the Body right.* Study I Corinthians 12:12—13:8 (about the Body of Christ, spiritual gifts, and loving one another). How has God provided for harmony in the Church? What is left for us to do?

2. *Don't give up the "ships."* List your church's activities, using a current bulletin for reference. Decide how each contributes to one or more of the four "ships"—fellowship, worship, stewardship, and discipleship. How would Christlike love aid the effectiveness of each of these activities?

Learning Obedience
1. *All we like sheep.* Study Psalm 23. How does the obedience of the sheep lead to the most satisfying life? What harm might disobedience cause? Is it difficult to see ourselves as sheep? To see Christ as the Good Shepherd?

2. *The Lord is my . . . .* Have group members rephrase Psalm 23, using a metaphor that means more to them than the sheep/shepherd comparison. Be sure to emphasize obedience, whatever the figure of speech.

Talking About Faith
1. *Witness in the desert.* Study the account of Philip's witness to the Ethiopian in Acts 8:26-39. What questions could have come up in Philip's mind during the experience? What did

125

Philip need to know in order to do what he did? How did Philip deal with the man's questions? How did he lead the man to make a commitment to Christ? What can we learn from Philip's example?

2. *Conversation pieces.* Brainstorm a list of recent news events, TV shows, fads, songs, and other pieces of popular culture that could be used as conversation starters in witnessing. Assign teams to act out conversations which start with these items and take a more personal, spiritual turn.

Living Christ Through the Week
1. *Servants and masters.* Read Ephesians 6:5-9. Who is the Christian's real "boss"? What does the Lord expect of employees? Supervisors? How does their Biblical relationship differ from the one usually observed in our culture? What would it mean for your group members to work "as unto Christ; not with eyeservice, as men-pleasers"?

2. *Wearing the armor.* Read Ephesians 6:10-18. With what principalities and powers do your group members wrestle during the week? What do the pieces of the whole armor of God represent? How would your students' weekday worlds be affected if they wore the armor each day? Have them describe situations in which each piece of armor would be especially useful.